Editor
Eric Migliaccio

Managing Editor
Ina Massler Levin, M.A.

Illustrator
Mark Mason

Cover Artist
Denise Bauer

Art Production Manager
Kevin Barnes

Imaging
James Edward Grace
Rosa C. See

Author

Susan R. Fineman, M.S.

Publisher
Mary D. Smith, M.S. Ed.

Teacher Created Resources, Inc.
6421 Industry Way
Westminster, CA 92683
www.teachercreated.com

ISBN: 978-1-4206-3971-1

©2006 Teacher Created Resources, Inc.
Reprinted, 2014

Made in U.S.A.

The classroom teacher may reproduce the materials in this book and/or CD for use in a single classroom only. The reproduction of any part of this book and/or CD for other classrooms or for an entire school or school system is strictly prohibited. No part of this publication may be transmitted or recorded in any form without written permission from the publisher with the exception of electronic material, which may be stored on the purchaser's computer only.

Table of Contents

Introduction

Read All About It! is a workbook that uses the newspaper to teach reading skills. Each reading comprehension exercise contained in this book is based on an Associated Press news story. The reading skill lessons are intended for students in grades 7 and 8. All teachers—including special-education teachers, resource teachers, remedial teachers, bilingual teachers, substitute teachers, parents, and nurses—will enjoy success using these exercises with their students. These nonfiction stories can be a terrific way to supplement a basic reading program and to inspire creative writing in your reading and writing classes.

Read All About It! is divided into the following four sections:

- **Vocabulary** (pages 4–37)

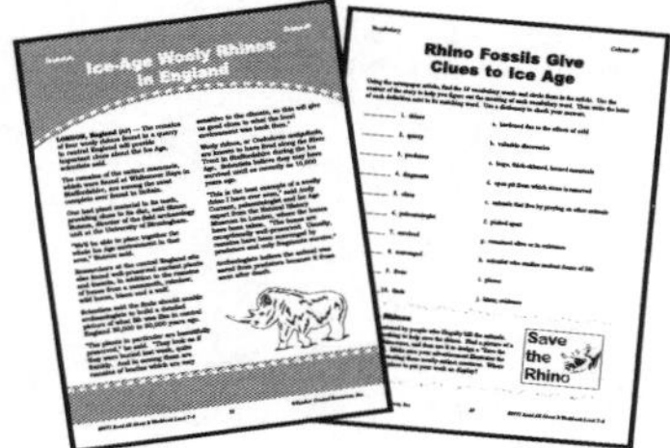
Ice-Age Wooly Rhinos in England

Rhino Fossils Give Clues to Ice Age

- **Question and Answers** (pages 38–71)

Post-It Notes Turn 20

Post-It Notes: Still Going Strong

- **Multiple Choice** (pages 72–105)

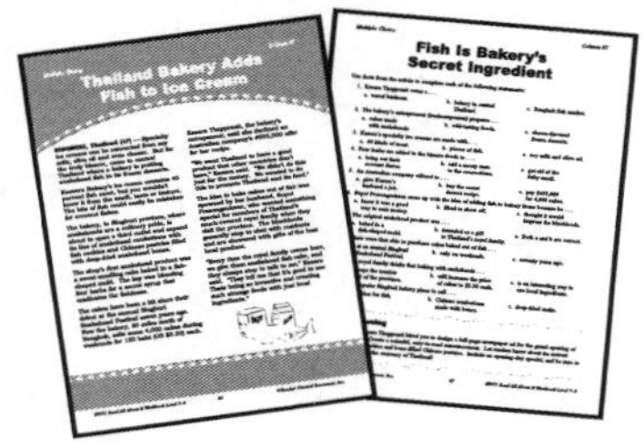
Thailand Bakery Adds Fish to Ice Cream

Fish Is Bakery's Secret Ingredient

- **True or False** (pages 106–139)

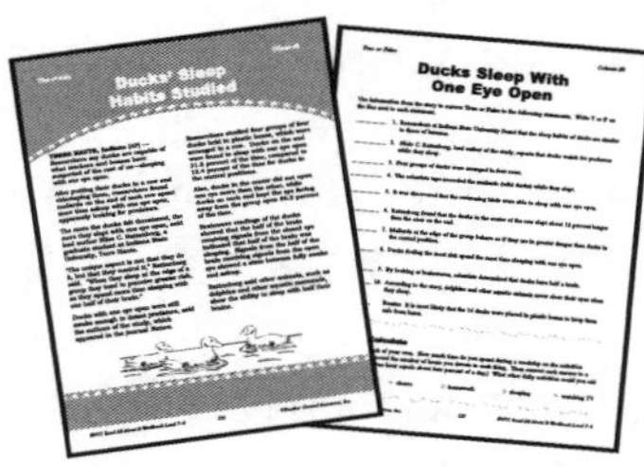
Ducks' Sleep Habits Studied

Ducks Sleep With One Eye Open

Each section contains 16 columns, complete with slightly-altered versions of the original Associated Press stories and the matching reading-comprehension exercises. The lessons are accompanied by easy-to-understand directions and specially designed worksheets. A progress plotter has been provided as a way for you to keep track of student achievement. In addition, each skill lesson is followed by a supplemental activity that expands upon the ideas in the article and encourages the students to make use of their new-found knowledge in a variety of creative ways.

At the beginning of each section is a list of instructions that are directed to the students. You may use all of them, some of them, or none of them. They are included as suggestions and as a way of helping students to understand the process required for mastery of each reading skill.

The lessons in *Read All About It!* may be followed in order or used individually. These exercises are classroom tested and offer a variety of topics that are appealing to students of all ability levels. They provide an innovative approach to the teaching of basic reading skills and help sustain enthusiasm for learning. The activities can be used to supplement and enrich basic reading curricula, to provide daily seatwork, to check for skill mastery, or to re-teach concepts. To assist in the correction of student work, a complete answer key is located in the back of the workbook

All materials used with permission from the Associated Press.

Vocabulary

General Directions

Before reading the article, list the vocabulary words on your worksheet, making sure to spell each word correctly. Next, find the 10 vocabulary words in the newspaper article and circle them. Use the context of the story to help you figure out or guess the meaning of each vocabulary word. Then select a meaning from the choices presented in the exercise, and record your answer next to the correct word. Use a dictionary to check your answers.

Suggested Directions to the Student

1. Read the headline to get a clue about the topic of the story.
2. Read the *entire* story, not just the parts containing the vocabulary words.
3. The words are usually not found in sequential order. You'll need to check the vocabulary list frequently when trying to locate words.
4. Use the context of the story to help you guess the meaning of a vocabulary word before selecting one of the choices listed in the exercise.
5. You may guess incorrectly. Therefore, when choosing an answer, consider all the meanings listed in the exercise, even if none of them resemble your definition.
6. Find the meanings of the vocabulary words you are most certain of first. That way you will have a better chance of matching the remaining definitions with the correct words.
7. Cross out each meaning after you record it next to the matching vocabulary word on the worksheet.
8. Only one of the meanings is right for each vocabulary word.
9. Be prepared to change your answers if you realize that a vocabulary word has been incorrectly matched with a meaning.
10. When checking for a dictionary definition, choose a meaning that fits the context of the story and is the same part of speech as the vocabulary word.
11. If a word ends in *s*, *ed*, or *ing*, look up the base word and adjust the meaning.
12. Use the supplemental activity to expand upon ideas presented in the story.

Vocabulary Worksheet

Student Name: ______________________________ Date: ______________

Column Title: ______________________________

Word List	Guess Using Context Clues	Meaning (Letter and Words)
1.		
2.		
3.		
4.		
5.		
6.		
7.		
8.		
9.		
10.		

Score Box

Lake's Long Name Puts Town on Map

WEBSTER, Mass. (AP) — Its blue waters and sparkling shoreline have been attracting vacationers for generations, but it's the sheer length of its name that has put Lake Char-gogg-a-gogg-man-chaugg-a-gogg-chau-bun-a-gun-ga-maugg on the map.

The Indian name is so long that it completely encircles window decals and fire truck doors and requires three wide traffic lanes to spell out at the entrance to the town beach and boat ramp.

"We're big on T-shirts and bumper stickers," says retired reporter Ed Patenaude.

Hundreds of tourists come to this central Massachusetts town of about 1,500 just to pose next to the signs. And the name—spelled various ways since the 1600s—has inspired poems, songs and tall tales.

The official town version has 45 letters (though one town sign painter got carried away and added a few extra). That makes it the longest lake name in the United States and one of the world's longest place names, according to the U.S. Geological Survey.

Ethel Merman and Ray Bolger paid homage to it in a song with a tom-tom in the 1920s. And calls come in to Town Hall from all over the world, demanding to know if it really exists and how to spell it.

When the state legislature tried to eliminate a few of the double g's in 1949, outraged residents squelched the scheme. The uproar promoted a Webster poet to write: "Should lofty redwoods not grow taller? Lo, as I live, the g-full name shall never grow smaller."

It's now a place of water skiers, dock parties and—in the winter—ice boat races.

Still, in the sleepy rhythm of a summer's day, visitors can sometimes hear an old recording of Merman and Bolger crooning:

"Oh, we took a walk one evening and we sat down on a log, by Lake Char-gogg-a-gogg-man-chaugg-a-gogg-chau-bun-a-gun-ga-maugg.

There we told loves old sweet story and we listened to a frog,

in Lake Char-gogg-a-gogg-man-chaugg-a-gogg-chau-bun-a-gun-ga-maugg."

 ©Teacher Created Resources, Inc.

Lake with Longest Name

Using the newspaper article, find the 10 vocabulary words and circle them in the article. Use the context of the story to help you figure out the meaning of each vocabulary word. Then write the letter of each definition next to its matching word. Use a dictionary to check your answers.

______ 1. sparkling	a. singing in a gentle manner
______ 2. homage	b. angered
______ 3. decals	c. pictures or designs transferred from specially prepared paper
______ 4. eliminate	d. put a stop to
______ 5. ramp	e. hold a position for a picture
______ 6. pose	f. special respect or honor
______ 7. outraged	g. sloping runway
______ 8. squelched	h. omit; take out
______ 9. version	i. glittering
______ 10. crooning	j. form or variation

Tell a Tall Tale

Suppose Webster town officials decided to hold a "tall tale" contest. You are invited to enter the competition by making up a story about how Lake Webster got its Indian name. Write your explanation in the form of prose, poetry, or song. Can you pronounce and spell Lake Webster's official name without looking?

Teens Rewarded After Turning in Money

TAMPA, Fla. (AP) — Two boys who found $4,000 in a paper bag in the street and turned it in were rewarded for their honesty with baseball tickets, honorary titles, keys to the city and other gifts.

"This must be worth $2,000," Jarvarious Jones said, as he looked at some of the gifts that officials and other lavished on him and Oscar Carter, both 13. They included baseball uniforms, bike helmets, gift certificates, shirts and an invitation to throw out the first pitch at a Tampa Devil Rays ball game.

The teenagers were made honorary prosecutors, policemen, Secret Service agents and sheriff's deputies. They also received a commendatory phone call from Gov. Jeb Bush.

"We're really proud of what you did," Bush said.

"I'm really surprised," said Oscar. "It makes me feel a lot special."

The teenagers found the dirty paper bag stuffed with $100 bills while waiting for their school bus. They thought about keeping the money, but instead turned it in when they arrived at school. Schoolmates teased them for not keeping it, they said.

"I knew I had to turn it in because it didn't belong to me," Jarvarious said.

"You have set an example for people of all ages," said Mark Ober, Hillsborough State Attorney.

Andrew Pride, a 72-year-old car salesman from Chicago, said he lost the cash during a golfing vacation and figured it was gone for good. Pride rewarded Oscar with a weekend shopping trip and gave money to Jarvarious.

Jacqueline Jones, Jarvarious's mother, said she was proud of her son.

"I always said to him to be honest, treat people as you want to be treated and if something isn't yours, find the owner," she said.

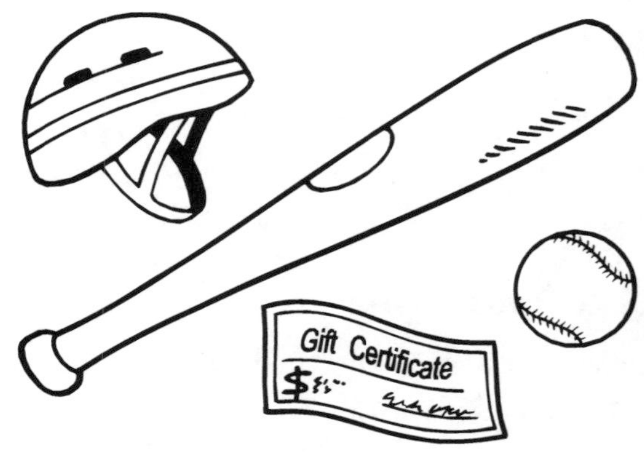

Teens Praised for Honesty

Using the newspaper article, find the 10 vocabulary words and circle them in the article. Use the context of the story to help you figure out the meaning of each vocabulary word. Then write the letter of each definition next to its matching word. Use a dictionary to check your answers.

________	1. honesty	a.	throw to the batter
________	2. figured	b.	truthfulness
________	3. commendatory	c.	heaped; piled
________	4. prosecutors	d.	made fun of
________	5. pitch	e.	protective head coverings
________	6. worth	f.	believed; thought
________	7. stuffed	g.	lawyers who bring cases against people accused of crimes
________	8. helmets	h.	equal in value to
________	9. teased	i.	crammed; filled
________	10. lavished	j.	praising

The Best Policy

Why do you think so many people rewarded Florida teens Jarvarious Jones and Oscar Carter? Of all the gifts they received, which do you think was the most appreciated by the two boys? What would you do if you found a bag stuffed with $100 bills? Be honest!

Quarter Depicts Helen Keller

BIRMINGHAM, Ala. (AP) — Helen Keller beat out a moon rocket, a Cherokee chief and other symbols for a spot on Alabama's state quarter, the first U.S. coin in circulation to include Braille.

Gov. Don Siegelman unveiled the design, which includes an image of Keller—an Alabama native who overcame blindness and deafness to become a writer and educator—reading a book in Braille.

Keller's name appears on the coin in both English and Braille, which has not previously been used on a U.S. coin in everyday use.

The quarter, which includes the slogan "Spirit of Courage," is intended to draw attention to education.

"I think it is fantastic," said Bill Johnson, a great-nephew of Keller's, who grew up in Tuscumbia, Alabama. "She was an amazing person."

The U.S. Mint made more than 650 million of the quarters, which went into circulation in March 2003.

School children submitted designs for the Alabama quarter, including a moon rocket or a space shuttle, to signify the state's contribution to the space program; Cherokee alphabet developer Sequoyah; and a Yellowhammer, the state bird.

Several students suggested a Keller coin, and a relative submitted a photo of her seated in a chair, reading, for the quarter. The governor picked Keller.

Born in 1880, Keller lost her sight and hearing to meningitis when she was a year old. With help from teacher Anne Sullivan, she learned to communicate with her hands and graduated from Radcliffe College. She died in 1968. Her life and Sullivan's struggle to help her were depicted in the play and movie *The Miracle Worker.*

The Keller coin was the 22nd quarter issued in the Mint's state quarters program, a 10-year project to salute all 50 states. Alabama was the 22nd state admitted to the Union.

The only U.S. coin to previously include Braille was an Olympic commemorative coin produced on a limited basis in the mid-1990s, said Mint spokesman Michael White.

Keller Symbolizes Courage

Using the newspaper article, find the 10 vocabulary words and circle them in the article. Use the context of the story to help you figure out the meaning of each vocabulary word. Then write the letter of each definition next to its matching word. Use a dictionary to check your answers.

__________ 1. image	a. short, catchy phrase
__________ 2. signify	b. struggled successfully against
__________ 3. spot	c. an illness in which infection swells the tissues covering the brain
__________ 4. admitted	d. allowed to join
__________ 5. overcame	e. exchange information and ideas
__________ 6. slogan	f. presented; offered
__________ 7. meningitis	g. recognize and honor
__________ 8. communicate	h. picture
__________ 9. submitted	i. represent
__________ 10. salute	j. place

Collectors' Items

The U.S. Mint began issuing commemorative state quarters in 1999. It's easy to find out which ones are circulating in your area. For the next week, ask family members and friends to look through their loose change for state quarters. Be prepared to trade an old-style quarter for a newly designed one. See how many different coins you can collect. Is your state's quarter in circulation?

Frozen Inca Child Studied

WASHINGTON, D.C. (AP) — A child sacrificed to the Inca gods and then preserved by mountaintop ice for about 500 years died of a powerful blow to the head, experts said.

The child, called Juanita by Peruvian scientists, is thought to be the best preserved body from pre-Columbian America ever discovered.

It was found still frozen in a ceremonial burial pit near the top of 20,700-foot Mount Ampato in Peru. The body has been kept in freezers since it was brought down from the mountain by American archaeologist Johan Reinhard. The remains went on display at the National Geographic Society building in Washington.

Dr. Elliot Fishman of Johns Hopkins University in Baltimore, head of a team that examined the body, said the girl died from a blow that shattered her skull just above her right eye.

"The cause of death was intercranial bleeding," Fishman said at a news conference.

He said the body was that of a well-nourished 12- to 14-year-old who was apparently in good health and of normal size.

"She has the best set of teeth that I've seen in many years," said Fishman.

He said a CT scan—a computer-driven X-ray device—clearly shows a crack in her skull and evidence that the brain was pushed to one side, probably as the result of bleeding within the skull.

Fishman said she probably did not regain consciousness after the blow and died within hours in the burial pit.

Reinhard said the child was dressed in fine clothes, including a rare feathered headdress, and then buried in a sitting position in a shallow pit near the summit of Mount Ampato, an inactive volcano near the town of Cabanaconde, Peru.

Children were sacrificed to the mountain gods by the Incas in the belief that the act would prevent bad events, such as volcanic eruptions, he said. Two other children were found near Juanita, but they were not as well preserved, he said.

The Incas ruled Peru for about 90 years, losing control in the Spanish conquest of 1533.

Frozen Teen Found

Using the newspaper article, find the 10 vocabulary words and circle them in the article. Use the context of the story to help you figure out the meaning of each vocabulary word. Then write the letter of each definition next to its matching word. Use a dictionary to check your answers.

__________	1. sacrificed	a. broke into pieces; smashed
__________	2. inactive	b. kept from decaying
__________	3. consciousness	c. hole in the ground
__________	4. archaeologist	d. a state of being awake and alert
__________	5. preserved	e. highest point
__________	6. shattered	f. temporarily still or quiet
__________	7. skull	g. a person who studies the life and culture of ancient people
__________	8. pit	h. killed as an offering (to a god, etc.)
__________	9. summit	i. bony framework of the head that encloses the brain
__________	10. shallow	j. not deep

Modern-Day Mementos

Juanita was buried along with jewelry, pots, and other artifacts of historical interest. Imagine that you could travel back in time to visit the Incas. What five items could you bring along that would help to explain present-day life and customs in America? Tell why you picked each one. Would you stay long?

Tiny Tiddleywink Back on Map

LONDON, England (AP) — After being virtually flicked from existence, the tiny but proud hamlet of Tiddleywink is back on the map.

The only sign pointing to the hamlet—a cluster of eight cottages in Wiltshire in southern England—was knocked over in a road accident four years ago, leading to confusion for postal and delivery workers.

Turning to the usual directories for assistance provided little help: the hamlet has been omitted from the current edition of the *Collins British Atlas and Gazetteer.*

Now Wiltshire County Council has put up two new name signs, much to the delight of local residents, who campaigned for its return.

"It's good news because people didn't know where we were. They were always having to ask the Post Office. But now we're back on the map," said Denis White, 79, who has lived in the hamlet for 40 years. "The name does make people smile. They usually say, 'What a lovely address.'"

Tiddleywink, which was in danger of being swallowed up by the neighboring village of Yatton Keynell, takes its name from the 18th-century use of the word for the children's game—now spelled tiddlywinks—as rhyming slang for "drinks."

The word evolved into slang for a small beer shop, such as the cottage in the hamlet that once served beer to passing cattle drovers.

"It's nice it has kept its name because people have lived here for years and it's a part of history," said Wiltshire County council member Jane Scott.

"It's also a great fun name and always makes me laugh. Apparently, when the old sign was up, Japanese and American visitors used to stop and have their photograph taken next to it—so goodness knows what will happen when the visitors come back in the summer."

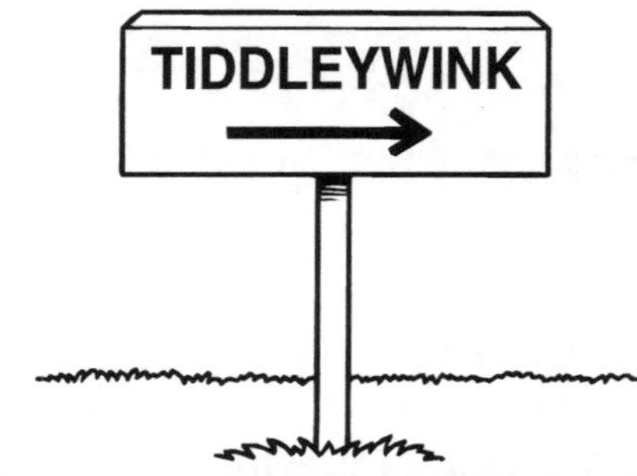

Tiny Town Gets Its Name Back

Using the newspaper article, find the 10 vocabulary words and circle them in the article. Use the context of the story to help you figure out the meaning of each vocabulary word. Then write the letter of each definition next to its matching word. Use a dictionary to check your answers.

________	1. cluster	a. latest; recent
________	2. assistance	b. developed gradually
________	3. flicked	c. struck with a quick, light blow
________	4. omitted	d. left out
________	5. hamlet	e. small village
________	6. slang	f. group
________	7. current	g. information
________	8. evolved	h. disorder; a mixed-up state
________	9. confusion	i. people who move herds of animals from one place to another
________	10. drovers	
		j. informal language used in place of standard words

Old-fashioned Fun

Tiddlywinks is just one of many classic children's games. Some others are jacks, pickup sticks, marbles, and hopscotch. Test your knowledge of these traditional fun activities by matching each game with one of the objects listed below. Have you ever played a game of tiddlywinks?

- box of chalk
- small rubber ball
- hard glass ball
- tapered piece of wood
- plastic disc

Museum's Elephant Gets Facelift

WASHINGTON, D.C. (AP) — Henry is back.

After months of being refurbished behind screens, the giant elephant that greets millions of visitors to the Smithsonian's National Museum of Natural History is back on public display.

Henry is the world's largest mounted creature—13 feet 2 inches tall at the shoulder. Henry has been moved only a few feet within the museum's rotunda, yet he seems transported thousands of miles, standing now in a display of the plants and animals of his native Africa.

Careful viewers may even notice, on a distant third-floor railing, a vulture staring down at the scene below.

Walking around Henry's new digs, called a diorama, the visitor can study the grasses of the Angolan savanna where the elephant once lived, and the birds and animals that shared the space with him.

Native African birds dot the display, fine examples of taxidermist's art. Included are a lilac-breasted roller, carmine bee eater and egrets.

In one corner, a jackal is crawling into his burrow. Moving around that corner the viewer can look into a small hole and see the mother jackal and her pups in their den, awaiting the male's arrival with food.

Other insects shown in the diorama include scarabs, robberflies and grassflies, and there are models of a lizard and a puff adder.

Since arriving in 1959, the elephant, unofficially known as Henry by the staffers, had been placed on a round platform, facing the entrance used by about 80 percent of the museum's 6 million annual visitors.

Now he is turned slightly and moved a few feet off center, his left tusk facing the main door.

How do you move a giant elephant? "Very carefully," responded Museum Director Robert Wi Fri, laughing. "It was one of the most stressful nights our head of exhibit construction has ever had."

 ©Teacher Created Resources, Inc.

Henry the Giant Elephant

Using the newspaper article, find the 10 vocabulary words and circle them in the article. Use the context of the story to help you figure out the meaning of each vocabulary word. Then write the letter of each definition next to its matching word. Use a dictionary to check your answers.

________ 1. refurbished	a. workers; assistants
________ 2. taxidermist	b. scene showing figures in a natural setting
________ 3. rotunda	c. dog-like mammal of Africa and Asia
________ 4. savanna	d. carried, moved
________ 5. transported	e. large bird with a featherless head
________ 6. staffers	f. long, pointed tooth
________ 7. vulture	g. flat plain with few trees
________ 8. diorama	h. large round hall
________ 9. tusk	i. person skilled in the art of stuffing and mounting the skins of dead animals
________ 10. jackal	j. freshened up; restored

Smithsonian Souvenir

Imagine that the Smithsonian asked you to design a lifelike poster of Henry in his natural habitat. Your creation would be sold in the museum's gift shop. Use facts from the story and pictures from an encyclopedia to help you design your poster. Remember, Henry is 13 feet 2 inches tall!

Carnegie Choir Is Dream Come True

NEW YORK, N.Y. (AP) — A high school girls' choir from Milwaukee made it all the way to the stage of Carnegie Hall, fulfilling a dream their teacher financed with the money she had saved for retirement.

The sacrifice was worth it, Nancy Ehlinger said, because her girls' performance "just shows that urban kids can be as good as suburban kids."

"It gives me a sense of accomplishment," she said before the concert. "I've been able to give the kids something they will never forget."

The teacher known to her students as Miss E received an invitation for the choir to perform with four other school groups at a concert in the famed concert hall.

She organized bake sales, a raffle and a lottery and wrote to 70 foundations to pay the travel expenses = $1,036 per girl for five days.

The fundraising brought in enough to pay the first $4,000 installment for the trip. But when the next two installments came due and only $1,250 had come from the foundations, she dug into her own future, borrowing $8,000 on two credit cards and withdrawing $28,680 from her IRA (Individual Retirement Account).

"I wanted the kids to have the opportunity," Miss E said. "I didn't want it to fly away."

Eventually, as news of her beneficence spread, the choir raised an additional $21,000, enabling her to put back most of what she'd withdrawn.

Twice, the last time in 1984, Miss E had performed at Carnegie Hall with the Milwaukee Symphony Chorus, an experience the 56-year-old teacher wanted to duplicate for her choir's inner-city teenagers.

"She is the most dedicated teacher I know," said Tiffany Lee, 16, a soprano. "She dedicated her time, her money, her spirits, everything—everything she could give us. In return, we gave her respect, a teacher award, a thank-you plaque, a sheet cake and balloons."

Choir Takes Unforgettable Trip

Using the newspaper article, find the 10 vocabulary words and circle them in the article. Use the context of the story to help you figure out the meaning of each vocabulary word. Then write the letter of each definition next to its matching word. Use a dictionary to check your answers.

________	1. duplicate	a. repeat; copy
________	2. dedicated	b. devoted
________	3. beneficence	c. flat piece of wood or metal with designs or lettering on one side
________	4. installment	d. kindness; good deed
________	5. accomplishment	e. widely known; famous
________	6. foundations	f. partial payment
________	7. financed	g. organizations set up to pay for charities
________	8. famed	h. achievement; something completed successfully
________	9. plaque	i. funded
________	10. choir	j. group of singers

Words of Praise

Think of a teacher you know who does a really good job. Imagine that this devoted teacher is to be honored at a school luncheon and that you are to be a guest speaker. Prepare for the occasion by writing a short speech about what makes this educator so special. Any suggestions for a gift?

Police to Target Unbuckled Children

WASHINGTON, D.C. (AP) — Children who are not buckled up are three times more likely to be seriously hurt in a traffic accident, according to a study released the same day police nationwide prepared to crack down on seat belt scofflaws.

"Unfortunately, motor vehicle crashes continue to be the leading cause of death and acquired disability in children over age 1 in this country," said Dr. Flaura K. Winston, the principal investigator for the study by The Children's Hospital of Philadelphia and State Farm Insurance.

Police from 8,100 agencies around the country plan to increase patrols and use seat belt checkpoints to target drivers transporting unbuckled kids. The effort is called Operation ABC Mobilization: America Buckles Up Children.

"Shame on the person who gets in the car and doesn't have more regard for that child's life," said Assistant Chief Terrance Gainer of the D.C. Metropolitan Police Department. "For the person who's so shameless, we're going to take them to jail or give them a ticket. We're going to help save your kids even if you won't."

In some states, citizens who know of motorists who don't buckle children can call a toll-free number to report them. The car's owner will be sent a letter about vehicle safety.

Every state has laws requring young children to either ride in car seats or wear seat belts.

"While the laws vary from state to state by what age and size child they cover, the laws of physics are the same everywhere," said Gerald Scannell, president of the National Safety Council. "Seat belts reduce the risk of death by 45 percent and reduce the risk of serious injury by 50 percent."

Among those at the news conference announcing the seat belt initiative was Edith Morgan, the mother of Derrick Thomas, a Kansas City Chiefs linebacker and All-Pro who died from injuries sustained in a car crash. Thomas was not wearing a seat belt.

The Professional Football Players' Association has begun "Buckle Up for 58" in honor of Thomas.

"For the child's safety, please buckle up because that's an important life you are playing with," Morgan said.

 ©Teacher Created Resources, Inc.

Buckle Up for Safety

Using the newspaper article, find the 10 vocabulary words and circle them in the article. Use the context of the story to help you figure out the meaning of each vocabulary word. Then write the letter of each definition next to its matching word. Use a dictionary to check your answers.

__________	1. scofflaws	a. decrease
__________	2. motorists	b. main; chief
__________	3. leading	c. people who drive automobiles
__________	4. reduce	d. aim at; pay special attention to
__________	5. patrols	e. written order to appear in court for breaking a traffic law
__________	6. target	f. suffered; experienced
__________	7. regard	g. people who regularly break the law
__________	8. risk	h. concern
__________	9. ticket	i. groups who watch an area
__________	10. sustained	j. possibility; chance

Concerned Citizens

In some states, citizens concerned about children not wearing seat belts can call a special hotline number. In those states, scofflaws will receive a notice about vehicle safety. Using facts from the story, write your own version of a warning letter. Explain why it's important to make sure children are buckled up. Do you practice what you preach?

Ice-Age Wooly Rhinos in England

LONDON, England (AP) — The remains of four wooly rhinos found in a quarry in central England will provide important clues about the Ice Age, scientists said.

The remains of the extinct mammals, which were found at Whitemoor Haye in Staffordshire, are among the most complete ever found in Britain.

One had plant material in its teeth, providing clues to its diet, said Simon Buteux, director of the field archaeology unit at the University of Birmingham.

"We'll be able to piece together the whole Ice Age environment in that area," Buteux said.

Researchers at the central England site also found well-preserved ancient plants and insects, in addition to the remains of bones from a mammoth, reindeer, wild horse, bison and a wolf.

Scientists said the finds should enable archaeologists to build a detailed picture of what life was like in central England 30,000 to 50,000 years ago.

"The plants in particular are beautifully preserved," he said. "They look as if they were buried last week, quite frankly. And in among them are remains of beetles which are very sensitive to the climate, so this will give us good clues to what the local environment was back then."

Wooly rhinos, or *Coelodonta antiquitatis,* are known to have lived along the River Trent in Staffordshire during the Ice Age. Scientists believe they may have survived until as recently as 10,000 years ago.

"This is the best example of a woolly rhino I have ever seen," said Andy Currant, paleontologist and Ice Age expert from the Natural History Museum in London, where the bones have been taken. "The bones are exceptionally well-preserved. Usually, remains have been scavenged by predators and only fragments survive."

Archeologists believe the animal was saved from predators because it froze soon after death.

Rhino Fossils Give Clues to Ice Age

Using the newspaper article, find the 10 vocabulary words and circle them in the article. Use the context of the story to help you figure out the meaning of each vocabulary word. Then write the letter of each definition next to its matching word. Use a dictionary to check your answers.

________	1. rhinos	a. hardened due to the effects of cold
________	2. quarry	b. valuable discoveries
________	3. predators	c. large, thick-skinned, horned mammals
________	4. fragments	d. open pit from which stone is removed
________	5. clues	e. animals that live by preying on other animals
________	6. paleontologist	f. picked apart
________	7. survived	g. remained alive or in existence
________	8. scavenged	h. scientist who studies ancient forms of life
________	9. froze	i. pieces
________	10. finds	j. hints; evidence

Save the Rhinos

Rhinos are threatened by people who illegally kill the animals. You can do something to help save the rhinos. Find a picture of a black or white rhinoceros, and then use it to design a "Save the Rhino" billboard. Make sure your advertisement illustrates the importance of protecting these nearly-extinct creatures. Where would be the best place to put your work on display?

Workers Find "Buffalo Bill" Billboard

JAMESTOWN, N.Y. (AP) — The crumbling brick façade of a downtown building revealed a long-forgotten secret: a 124-year-old billboard promoting a dramatic appearance by "Buffalo Bill" Cody.

Experts say the 26-by-10-foot billboard, uncovered when workers began removing the wall last month to prevent its collapse, is among the earliest graphic representations of the Wild West legend.

Pasted to wood sheathing behind the bricks was the paper poster of Cody waving his hat to a crowd, announcing: "Buffalo Bill in his new theatrical drama...May Cody" on March 14, 1878.

"We knew we had to act quickly," said Keith Schmitt, acting director of the Chautauqua County Arts Council, which quickly began preservation work on the fragile paper. "Some of the pieces were already coming away from the wall and blowing away."

Schmitt and volunteers photographed the pieces and collected those that were removable as historians began researching the performance at the Allen Opera House in this city 60 miles south of Buffalo.

Historian Karen Livsey found that the show was part of a sixth-anniversary tour of The Buffalo Bill Combination, an early theater troupe organized by and starring Cody. "May Cody" depicted the Mormons' early settlement in Utah.

Experts believe the wall was built over the poster the year of the performance, hiding it ever since.

William F. Cody, who died in 1917, was a prospector-turned-Pony Express rider and Civil War veteran who later hunted buffalo to feed railroad construction crews. It is said that he earned the right to the name "Buffalo Bill" in a day-long shooting match with a hunter named William Comstock, presumably to determine who deserved the title.

Cody became a national folk hero in the pages of the "Buffalo Bill" dime novels of Ned Buntline, who in 1872 persuaded Cody to take to the stage to tell stories of the Wild West. The Buffalo Bill Combination toured the country for 10 years until 1883, when Cody began the Wild West Show.

 ©Teacher Created Resources, Inc.

Poster of Cowboy Hero Found

Using the newspaper article, find the 10 vocabulary words and circle them in the article. Use the context of the story to help you figure out the meaning of each vocabulary word. Then write the letter of each definition next to its matching word. Use a dictionary to check your answers.

________	1. facade	a.	famous person admired for a skill or talent
________	2. match	b.	easily damaged; delicate
________	3. collapse	c.	presentation before an audience; show
________	4. legend	d.	front face or wall
________	5. prospector	e.	person looking for valuable minerals
________	6. billboard	f.	group of traveling performers
________	7. troupe	g.	urged; convinced
________	8. fragile	h.	large advertising sign
________	9. persuaded	i.	falling down suddenly
________	10. performance	j.	contest

"Buffalo Bill" Biography

There's lots of interesting information about William F. Cody in this article. Read the story again, and see if you can list 10 facts about the cowboy hero. Then look in an encyclopedia for five more details to add to your "biography" of the Wild West legend. If you could ask "Buffalo Bill" one question, what would it be?

Solar System Emerges Along Maine Highway

PRESQUE ISLE, Maine (AP) — For drivers zipping along U.S. 1, it's easy to overlook planet Mars. After all, it's only 3 inches in diameter, perched atop a pole next to the "Welcome to Presque Isle" sign.

But it's hard to miss Jupiter, which is 5 feet in diameter and weighs closer to a ton, next to a potato field.

What unfolds on a stretch of a highway through the rolling farm country of northern Maine is billed as the world's largest scale model of the solar system.

"There's a sense of pride," said Kevin McCartney, a geology professor at the University of Maine at Presque Isle. "You could not build something like this in 99.9 percent of the United States."

The center of this solar system is the university where McCartney works. Driving south on U.S. 1, it ends 40 miles later with tiny Pluto mounted on the wall of a visitor information center in Houlton.

At scale, 7 mph would be the equivalent of driving at the speed of light; it would take eight minutes to travel from the sun to Earth. Of course, that would be ill-advised on a two-lane highway.

Because the planets were built to scale, it can be something of a game of hide and seek to find the smaller ones.

Earth, which is a bit larger than a softball, is located next to the Chrysler-Jeep-Dodge sign at Percy's Auto Sales. Venus, at 5 inches in diameter, is in a motel parking lot. Mercury, at 2 inches, is in a garden by the highway.

Pluto, the smallest, is an inch in diameter.

Seven of the planets are surrounded by moons, most of which are attached to metal rods that are stuck in the ground.

"The larger planets really make a statement. The small ones are hard to locate," said Tom Cote, an art instructor at Limestone Community School who enlisted students to help paint Jupiter.

Cote supervised students from kindergarten to high school who painted the massive planet over a six-month period.

The students pored over photographs provided by NASA's Jet Propulsion Laboratory and mixed acrylic paints to get the hues of pink, orange and red, said Jacinda St. Pierre, a high school junior.

"In the end, it was quite an accomplishment to finish it and have it look as good as it did."

 ©Teacher Created Resources, Inc.

Maine Town Puts Planets on Display

Using the newspaper article, find the 10 vocabulary words and circle them in the article. Use the context of the story to help you figure out the meaning of each vocabulary word. Then write the letter of each definition next to its matching word. Use a dictionary to check your answers.

________	1. perched	a. large and/or heavy
________	2. scale	b. advertised
________	3. zipping	c. straight, thin sticks
________	4. billed	d. miss; fail to notice
________	5. overlook	e. sitting; placed
________	6. unfolds	f. colors
________	7. enlisted	g. accurately proportioned
________	8. massive	h. traveling quickly; speeding
________	9. rods	i. extends; becomes visible
________	10. hues	j. signed up; arranged for

Planetary Probe

Can you list the nine planets in order of their distance from the sun? Use an encyclopedia to check your work and to write down two or three distinguishing characteristics of each celestial body. Find out which is the second largest planet, which have polar ice caps, and which takes about 248 years to revolve around the sun. Which is the only planet known to support life?

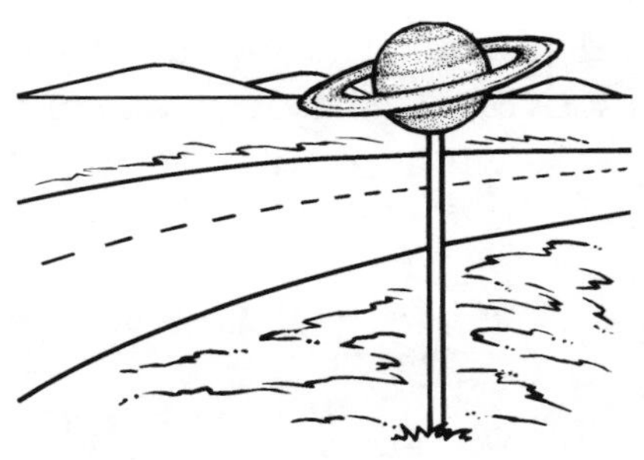

Crocodiles May Have Been 30 Feet Long

WASHINGTON, D.C. (AP) — A giant dinosaur-munching crocodile that grew to 30 feet in length and tipped the scales at 10,000 pounds achieved its gargantuan proportions by sheer longevity, new research suggests.

Eighty million-year-old fossils of *Deinosuchus*, or "Terror Crocodile," contain annual growth layers like tree rings in the bony, armor-like plates that lined the saltwater reptile's back and sides.

Microscopic analysis of those bones suggest *Deinosuchus* was a slow-grower like modern crocs, but grew much larger by living to about 50 years—some two decades longer, paleontologist Gregory M. Erickson said.

"You either grow very fast like the dinosaurs or take the slow road and extend your development over a long period of time. That's what these animals did. They just prolonged their growth," said Erickson, a postdoctoral fellow in mechanical engineering at Stanford University.

The first *Deinosuchus* remains—teeth and pieces of a skull and jaw—were discovered in North Carolina in 1858. But it wasn't until 1909, after larger finds in Texas and Montana, that the fossils were described as belonging to a giant extinct crocodile.

Still, what emerged from the fossil record was more like an alligator than a crocodile. It had a broad, flat alligator-like snout unlike most crocs' thin narrow snouts, said Brochu, a postdoctoral research scientist at the Field Museum.

And that huge snout was lined with dagger-like teeth 5 to 6 inches in length that are similar to those wielded by *Tyrannosaurus rex.*

While T-Rex ruled the land, *Deinosuchus* (pronounced DINE-oh-sue-cuss) loomed large along the estuaries and shores of a shallow tropical sea that covered much of North America's present interior. It probably dined on dinosaurs, though teeth marks found on fossil shells of giant sea turtles suggest it was also on the terror crocodile's menu.

But *Deinosuchus*'s reign during the late Cretaceous period was brief—only about 10 million years. They became extinct about 80 million years ago, perhaps falling victim to their inability to slake their enormous appetites.

 ©Teacher Created Resources, Inc.

Terror Crocodile

Using the newspaper article, find the 10 vocabulary words and circle them in the article. Use the context of the story to help you figure out the meaning of each vocabulary word. Then write the letter of each definition next to its matching word. Use a dictionary to check your answers.

__________	1. slake	a. possessed and used
__________	2. annual	b. huge; enormous
__________	3. gargantuan	c. yearly
__________	4. estuaries	d. wide lower part of rivers
__________	5. longevity	e. ability to live long
__________	6. munching	f. satisfy
__________	7. lined	g. covered the inner surface of
__________	8. snout	h. periods of ten years
__________	9. decades	i. long nose and jaws
__________	10. wielded	j. chewing; eating

Measuring Up

Scientists believe that a young "Terror Crocodile" had growth spurts of almost a foot a year. What's your growth rate? How much have you grown in the past 12 months? Do you grow the same amount every year? By age 18, how tall do you expect to be? Why? How long were you when you were born?

Grave Is One of Europe's Richest

LONDON, England (AP) — A 4,000-year-old grave found near Stonehenge contains the remains of an archer and a trove of artifacts that make it one of the richest early Bronze Age sites in Europe, archaeologists said.

"It's a fantastically important discovery both for the number of artifacts found in that grave and the range of artifacts. It's absolutely unique," said Gillian Varndell, a curator of the British Museum's prehistory department.

About 100 objects, including a pair of rare gold earrings, were found three miles east of Stonehenge with the bones of a man who died at about the time the monolithic stone circle was taking the form we see today.

"It is the single richest burial from the British Isles at about this date," said Andrew Fitzpatrick, the Wessex Archaeology project manager in charge of the site at Amesbury, 75 miles southwest of London.

"Previously, if seven or eight objects had been placed in the grave, we would have thought that person quite wealthy and highly regarded," Fitzpatrick said. "Here, we have getting-on-for 100. It's much bigger than anything we could have imagined."

The man has been identified as an archer because the objects buried with him included stone arrowheads and stone wristguards that protected the arm from the recoil of the bow.

There also were stone tools for butchering carcasses and for making more arrowheads.

As well as the archery equipment, the man had three copper knives and a pair of gold earrings, Fitzpatrick said. He said the archaeologists believe the earrings were wrapped around the ear rather than hanging from the ear lobe.

He described the earrings as among the earliest kinds of metal object found in Britain.

"They were very rare and the metals they were made from may have been imported," he said.

The burial, in about 2300 B.C., occurred at "the very brink of the Bronze Age," where Neolithic and metal-using societies meet, Varndell said. It was a stage when people were using copper and sheet gold, and were about to learn how to use complicated metals.

 ©Teacher Created Resources, Inc.

Bronze Age Grave a Unique Find

Using the newspaper article, find the 10 vocabulary words and circle them in the article. Use the context of the story to help you figure out the meaning of each vocabulary word. Then write the letter of each definition next to its matching word. Use a dictionary to check your answers.

__________	1. butchering	a. guessed; thought
__________	2. monolithic	b. objects made by humans
__________	3. archer	c. sudden backward movement
__________	4. imagined	d. bodies of dead animals
__________	5. wealthy	e. person who shoots with a bow and arrow
__________	6. artifacts	f. massive; huge
__________	7. trove	g. slaughtering and preparing for food
__________	8. recoil	h. rich
__________	9. imported	i. valuable collection
__________	10. carcasses	j. brought in from another country

The Amesbury Archer

The 4,000-year-old grave is described as "a fantastically important discovery." Make some gravesite discoveries of your own on the Net at *www.wessexarch.co.uk/projects/amesbury/archer.html.* Begin by clicking on the words "The Finds" to see pictures of the archer's copper knives, weapons, gold earring, and wristguards. Then return to the home page and continue to "dig" for information. Are you impressed with the "trove of artifacts?"

Early Reference to Baseball Found

NEW YORK, N.Y. (AP) — The quest to nail down the origins of baseball has been thrown a curve with the discovery of two newspaper articles showing the game was played earlier than historians thought.

The articles appeared on April 25, 1823, and show that an organized form of a game called "base ball" was being played in Manhattan, in what is today Greenwich Village.

The articles were discovered by George A. Thompson Jr., a librarian at New York University. Historians have long wrestled with the task of discovering the true origins of the game—and whether it was invented or simply evolved.

For decades, the widely accepted version was that Maj. Gen. Abner Doubleday dreamed up the game in 1839 while a cadet at West Point and later encouraged it among his Union troops during the Civil War.

The legend led to the founding of the National Baseball Hall of Fame in Doubleday's home town of Cooperstown, New York, although later evidence pointed to the first real game being played in Hoboken, New Jersey, in 1846.

Last fall, Thompson was poking through the pages of the long-forgotten *National Advocate* when he discovered a brief item from 1823 referring to Saturday games of "base ball" at what is now Broadway and Eighth Street in lower Manhattan.

The writer, calling himself "A Spectator," was "much pleased in witnessing a company of active young men playing the manly and athletic game" and said another contest was to be held on the same field a week later.

The same day, the *New-York Gazette and General Advertiser* carried a one-paragraph item saying it had "received a communication in favor of the manly exercise of base ball," presumably from the same "Spectator."

"When I found the item, I was struck by the fact that the game was 'base ball,' and that it had to be a very early reference, if not the earliest," Thompson said.

The newspapers saw no need to explain what "base ball" was, Thompson noted, suggesting that many people were already familiar with the game.

"They took it for granted that people would understand what it was about," he said.

 ©Teacher Created Resources, Inc.

Baseball's Beginnings

Using the newspaper article, find the 10 vocabulary words and circle them in the article. Use the context of the story to help you figure out the meaning of each vocabulary word. Then write the letter of each definition next to its matching word. Use a dictionary to check your answers.

______	1. origins		a. slowly searching
______	2. legend		b. job
______	3. organized		c. developed gradually
______	4. poking		d. struggled; had difficulty
______	5. reference		e. beginnings
______	6. witnessing		f. story passed down from earlier times
______	7. cadet		g. well thought-out; arranged
______	8. task		h. written comment
______	9. evolved		i. seeing
______	10. wrestled		j. student training to become a member of the military

Baseball Greats

Below is a list of six baseball players who were inducted into the National Baseball Hall of Fame. Read about each of these amazing athletes on the Net at *www.baseballhalloffame.org*. Click on Hall of Famers and then on Hall of Fame roster. Who was the first to be voted into the Hall of Fame? Which player would you want on your team, and why?

- Roberto Clemente
- Sandy Koufax
- Willie Mays
- Jackie Robinson
- Babe Ruth
- Lou Gehrig

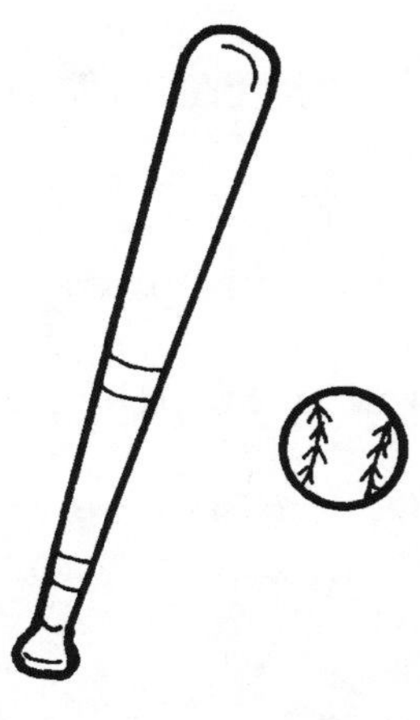

Clown College Holds Reunion

LAS VEGAS, Nev. (AP) — The man with the bulbous red nose, his friend on stilts with the huge blue feet and striped pants and the woman with canary yellow hair have a lot in common.

They were among some 300 alumni of the Ringling Bros. and Barnum & Bailey Clown College who reunited to snap photos and swap stories at—appropriately—the Circus-Circus hotel-casino on the Las Vegas Strip.

"My family and friends said all my life I was born a clown," said Joe Strange, 44, who says he joined the class of 1984 because he wanted to live up to his name. "Then I was going to school in theater, bugging the teachers to do comedy and they said, "Why don't you go to clown college?"

The tuition-free clown college based in Venice, Florida, produced more than 1,500 graduates from its opening in 1968—when the profession seemed to be dwindling—until it closed in 1997.

"Basically we had trained more clowns than we could hire at that point in time," said Peggy Williams of the class of 1970.

Clown school wasn't just for laughs. Students worked and lived with each other around the clock eight and a half weeks before the "Big Show," which served as their final exam. While no one failed, it was their chance to prove themselves and be chosen to tour with Ringling Bros.

"I think clowning will be around whether there's a formal institution to teach it or not because it's been around for centuries," said Dawn Pollock Jones, who earned a degree in theater from Northwestern University before attending clown school. "It's going to stay around because everyone likes to have fun."

Others worry theirs is art form in transition.

"We don't know if it's going to go up or down," Strange said. "It's like the stock market."

After nine years of traveling with three different circuses, Strange now operates a dinner theater in Indianapolis.

Since the college shut down its training rings, Ringling Bros. is calling former graduates to come back to the circus tent, Strange said.

"I got a call from the boss of the red unit saying 'Are you sure you don't want to come back?' It sure was tempting because that's your family," he said. "But I got tired of being on the road."

Clowns in Town

Using the newspaper article, find the 10 vocabulary words and circle them in the article. Use the context of the story to help you figure out the meaning of each vocabulary word. Then write the letter of each definition next to its matching word. Use a dictionary to check your answers.

________ 1. stilts	a. exchange; trade
________ 2. alumni	b. came together again
________ 3. swap	c. a pair of long poles with foot supports used for walking above the ground
________ 4. tour	d. growing smaller; shrinking
________ 5. reunited	e. pestering; annoying
________ 6. centuries	f. appealing; attractive
________ 7. dwindling	g. the process of changing
________ 8. transition	h. graduates; former students
________ 9. bugging	i. hundreds of years
________ 10. tempting	j. travel from place to place to perform

Just for Laughs

If you're looking for fun, you've found it! Step right up and explore the Ringling Bros. website at *www.ringling.com/activity/clownfun/*. Begin by clicking on the words "Create A Clown," where you can design thousands of funny faces. Next, go back and try "Morph A Clown." Would you make a good clown? Choose "Aptitude Test" from the sidebar and find out!

"Killer" Sponges Lurk in Caves

NEW YORK, N.Y. (AP) — From a dark cave in the Mediterranean Sea comes a tale of sponges gone bad.

They left behind the placid feeding ways of other sponges, which filter seawater to pull out bacteria and other microscopic snacks. That wasn't enough for them.

They became Killer Sponges.

They capture and eat small shrimps and similar creatures up to a quarter-inch long, which can struggle vainly for hours to escape. For a sponge, that's like bagging big game.

Their secret was discovered by scientists Nicole Boury-Esnault and Jean Vacelet of the Oceanographic Center of Marseille in France.

Killer sponges may also lurk elsewhere, including deep in the Atlantic and Pacific Oceans, Vacelet said.

Sponges are animals that anchor themselves to rocks or other solid objects, usually in oceans. Each sponge is basically a collection of cells on a natural scaffold. It has no internal organs like a heart or lung.

The killer sponges grow about three-quarters of an inch tall, with a white oval body at the end of a thread-like stalk. Although they belong to a kind of sponge that normally lives very deep in the ocean, they apparently felt at home in the darkness and constant temperature of their shallow underwater cave near Marseille.

The sponges snag their prey in sticky threads that extend from their bodies. As the hapless creatures struggle, they bump up against more and more threads, which further entrap them.

It's not clear just how the prey finally dies, but perhaps it is smothered by the threads, Vacelet said.

Once the prey is dead, the sponge grows out at the capture site to engulf it. The meal is then digested, which takes up to eight days. Then the sponge extends its threads again, "ready for new prey," Vacelet said.

Killer sponges apparently evolved because the usual strategy of filtering seawater was just not getting enough food in the deep ocean, the researchers said.

Sponges are known to be highly adaptable, but the new study is the first to show they can eat animals.

The discovery should not make people squeamish if they use natural sponges at home. For one thing, the home product is just a sponge skeleton; it isn't a killer sponge.

 ©Teacher Created Resources, Inc.

Sponge Attack

Using the newspaper article, find the 10 vocabulary words and circle them in the article. Use the context of the story to help you figure out the meaning of each vocabulary word. Then write the letter of each definition next to its matching word. Use a dictionary to check your answers.

________	1. lurk	a. calm
________	2. microscopic	b. stem of a plant
________	3. placid	c. catch
________	4. adaptable	d. able to change easily
________	5. squeamish	e. lie hidden and ready to attack
________	6. stalk	f. developed gradually
________	7. constant	g. always the same
________	8. snag	h. very small
________	9. hapless	i. unfortunate; unlucky
________	10. evolved	j. feel sick in the stomach

Fishing for Facts

Many interesting animals live underwater. These sea creatures catch, capture, trap, or snag their prey in different ways. Be a science reporter. Choose one of the water animals listed below and write a story explaining how the animal gets its food. Give your article a "catchy" headline.

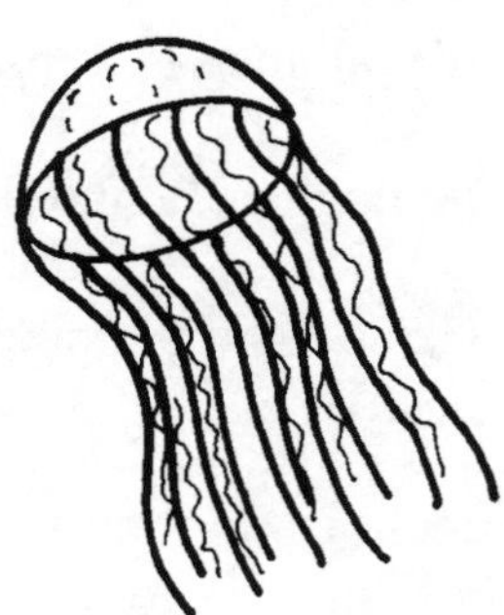

- jellyfish
- octopus
- sea anemone
- sea cucumber
- starfish
- squid

Questions and Answers

General Directions

Use the information from the Associated Press articles to answer the 10 questions. Write the answers on the lines provided below each question, or record the answers on the "Questions and Answers Worksheet" (page 39).

Suggested Directions to the Student

1. Read the headline to get a clue about the topic of the story.
2. Number the paragraphs. Whenever possible, find paragraph proof for your answers. (Exceptions include questions that ask for your opinion.)
3. You can either read the story first and then answer the questions or read the questions first to see what types of answers are required.
4. Use the context of the story to figure out the meaning of unfamiliar words.
5. All questions are based on the story. No additional text is needed to answer the questions.
6. Answers to questions are usually not found in sequential order in the story. (Ask, "Where in the story was the author looking when she wrote this question?")
7. If possible, begin your answer sentence with words from the question.
8. When writing answer sentences, avoid the use of pronouns.
9. After writing your sentence(s), use a highlighter or marker to underline the specific words or ideas that answer the question.
10. For inferential questions, make sure your answer makes sense and fits with the context of the story.
11. If you answer "Yes" or "No," be sure to explain your opinion.
12. Write clearly and don't write in the margins of your paper.
13. Use the supplemental activity to expand upon ideas presented in the story.

Teacher's Note: Make extra copies of the "Questions and Answers Worksheet" on page 39 for your students to use.

Questions and Answers Worksheet

Name: ____________________ Date: ______________________________

Story Title: __________________________

	Paragraph Proof	Answer
1.		
2.		
3.		
4.		
5.		
6.		
7.		
8.		
9.		
10.		

Smelly T. Rex on Display in London

LONDON, England (AP) — A new model of *Tyrannosaurus rex* unveiled Tuesday is something to sniff at.

Not content with just showing another replica dinosaur that moves and roars, the Natural History Museum wanted to capture the authentic smell of the fearsome beast. It wanted the whiff of a killer drenched in the blood of its prey, reeking of rotten meat and scarred with infected wounds.

And then it chickened out.

"We investigated a number of smells at first, but the reality of the smell of dead, rotting flesh was so off-putting, we figured we should go with the smell of the T-rex's environment instead of its breath," said Audrey O'Connell, head of international business at the museum.

The result, called Maastrichtian Miasma, is a boggy, acrid, earthy scent.

Dale Air Deodorising Ltd. of Lytham in northern England, which created the scent for the museum, specializes in aromas for museums, zoos and businesses.

"It took us about a month to do the dinosaur smell," company owner Frank Knight said at the Natural History Museum's unveiling of the T-rex.

The scent will waft around the 23-foot-long, 13.5-foot-high model, made at a cost of $330,000 by the Kokoro Co. of Japan.

So what will visitors miss by not getting a whiff of the dinosaur?

"The T-rex would have to be the most putrid, foulest thing that ever lived. A hyena times 10 would not even get you close," said Jack Horner, curator of paleontology at the Museum of the Rockies in Bozeman, Montana.

"The bigger you are, the stinkier you are, the nastier you are, the less other animals will mess with you."

T-rex lived about 65 to 68 million years ago in what is now western North America, Horner said.

It could run up to 25 mph on its three-clawed feet, and tore into its prey with 50 serrated teeth, each 6 inches long. Dinner included duckbilled dinosaurs, triceratops and other plant-eating creatures, and T-rex's digestive system had no problem with chunks of bone and horn.

Sniff-a-Dinosaur Exhibit

Use information from the article on page 40 to answer the following questions:

1. Why do you think London's Natural History Museum was not satisfied with its existing dinosaur display? ______________________________

2. How did the museum change its model of *Tyrannosaurus rex?* ______________________________

3. Name three things that could have made the killer beast smell putrid (rotten).

4. On which prehistoric animals did T-rex prey? ______________________________

5. In paragraph three, what does the expression "chickened out" mean? ______________________________

6. According to Audrey O'Connell, why did the museum decide not to use the true-to-life aroma of the huge animal? ______________________________

7. How does paleontologist Jack Horner describe the fearsome creature's odor?

8. It took Dale Air Deodorizing Ltd. a month to create the dinosaur scent. What does it smell like?

9. If you had to choose between using the smell of T-Rex's surroundings or its breath, which would you pick? Explain. ______________________________

10. Would you like to get a whiff of the "foulest thing that ever lived?" Explain.

New and Improved T-rex

Imagine that the Natural History Museum hired you to design an advertising leaflet for the "smelly dinosaur" exhibit. They plan to send your folded flyer to people who request information about the new display. Create a pamphlet that contains a picture of a T-rex, along with information about the creature and its nasty odor.

Japanese Unhappy with Plan to Cancel Classes

TOKYO, Japan (AP) — A bit more leeway in Japan's notoriously strict school system would seem to be a blessing, but few are cheering the plan to give children more days off.

Teachers, students, and parents are objecting to a plan to make public schools cancel classes two Saturdays per month. Students are now off one Saturday per month.

"It's hard enough to digest the current curriculum in a six-day week—a five-day week is ridiculous," said Mitsuo Arai, headmaster of a Tokyo high school.

Japanese children attend school about 240 days a year, compared with an average 180 in the United States. The Education Ministry decided to reduce the number of days, but not the hours kids have to spend in class. The time lost on Saturdays will have to be made up, possibly cutting into time for activities, sports and free time.

Several mothers interviewed on television shows voiced concerns about the extra burden of watching the kids.

"If the children are in school, I have more freedom in organizing my schedule and doing errands. But if they're off, I have to spend all the time taking care of them," one mother said.

An Education Ministry survey showed 47 percent of parents were opposed to the change, mostly because "the kids would only play more."

But that's the whole point, says the Education Ministry. In recent years the Education Ministry has tried to respond to accusations that Japan's schools produce regimented thinkers, but not the creative individualists a modern Japan needs.

Even some children interviewed were not especially happy with the new five-day week. Some said they would merely spend the extra time sleeping.

One elementary school student in a schoolyard said he would rather go to school on Saturdays.

"School is fun," he said.

 ©Teacher Created Resources, Inc.

School Days

Use information from the article on page 42 to answer the following questions:

1. How is the Japanese government planning to change the public school schedule?

2. In Japan, about how many days per week do children go to school?

3. Compared with American students, about how many more days a year do Japanese children attend school?

4. Who decides the number of days in the Japanese school year?

5. Why is Mitsuo Arai opposed to shortening the school week?

6. According to the article, what is one thing that will not change if the plan goes into effect?

7. Do you think that Japanese students spend more time studying than American students? Explain.

8. Name some ways that children in Japan might have to make up for time lost on Saturdays.

9. Why are so many Japanese parents unhappy about the plan to cancel Saturday classes?

10. Why do you think that some children might want to spend their free time sleeping?

Going Places

Pretend that you and a friend have decided to spend the weekend together. Plan your activities by turning to the entertainment section of your local paper. How about going to a sports event, the movies, a museum, or a restaurant? List the things you plan to do and show the time for each activity.

Super Ant Colony Found in Europe

WASHINGTON, D.C. (AP) — A supercolony of ants has been discovered stretching thousands of miles from the Italian Rivera along the coastline of northwest Spain.

It's the largest cooperative unit ever recorded, according to Swiss, French and Danish scientists, whose findings appear in the Proceedings of the National Academy of Sciences.

The 3,600-mile colony consists of billions of Argentine ants living in millions of nests that cooperate with one another.

Usually, ants from different nests fight. But the researchers concluded that ants in the supercolony were all close enough genetically to recognize one another, despite being from different nests with different queens.

Cooperation allows the colonies to develop at much higher densities than typically would occur, eliminating some 90 percent of other types of ants that live near them, said Laurent Keller of the University of Lausanne, Switzerland.

The Argentine ants were accidentally introduced to Europe around 1920, probably in ships carrying plants, Keller said.

Richard D. Fell, an entomologist at Virginia Polytechnic Institute, said Argentine ants have been known to form large colonies—the size of several city blocks, for example—but he had not heard of any as large as that cited in the new report.

"It may be that certain ant colonies will bud off, form satellites and remain connected with one main colony," he suggested.

The European researchers said that in addition to the main supercolony of ants they found a second, smaller but also large colony of Argentine ants in Spain's Catalonia region.

When ants from the two supercolonies were placed together, they invariably fought to the death, while ants from different nests of the same supercolony showed no aggression to each other.

"It is interesting to see that introduction in a new habitat can change social organization," Keller said of the behavior of Argentine ants that had been relocated to Europe. "In this case, this leads to the greatest cooperative unit ever discovered."

 ©Teacher Created Resources, Inc.

Scientists Find World's Largest Ant Colony

Use information from the article on page 44 to answer the following questions:

1. Where in the world have scientists discovered the largest supercolony of ants ever recorded?
2. How many miles long is the ant colony? How many ants form the record-breaking unit?
3. Before seeing the new report, how might entomologist Richard D. Fell have described the size of an Argentine ant colony?
4. How do you think researchers found the giant ant colony?
5. According to expert Laurent Keller, how were the Argentine ants introduced into Europe?
6. Why is the supercolony described as a "cooperative unit"?
7. Why are these tiny creatures able to live together so peacefully?
8. Where did European researchers find a second, smaller supercolony of Argentine ants?
9. What happened when ants from the two large colonies were placed together?
10. Keller says that putting Argentine ants in a new habitat can change their "social organization." What does he mean?

Fruit Fly Invasion

Even with strict plant quarantine laws, unwanted insects have been accidentally introduced into the United States. The Mediterranean fruit fly is one such pest. Look in an encyclopedia to find out more about this highly-destructive bug. How did the Medfly find its way into this country? Where has it been spotted? How is it controlled? Have you ever been pestered by a fruit fly?

Collapse of Mountain Saddens Locals

FRANCONIA, N.H. (AP) — New Hampshire awoke one Saturday to find its stern granite symbol of independence and stubborness, the Old Man of the Mountain, had collapsed into rubble.

The fall ended nearly a century of efforts to protect the giant mountainside landmark from the same natural forces that created it. Only stabilizing cables and epoxy remained where the famous ledges had clung.

"There's only so much you can do," said Mike Pelchat, a state parks official who hiked up the mountain after the collapse was discovered to make sure there were no signs of foul play.

"With heavy rains and high winds and freezing temperatures, the combination was just right to loosen him up," he said. "We always thought it was the hand of God holding him up, and He let go."

It was unclear when the outcropping actually fell from Cannon Mountain because clouds had obscured the area for a couple of days. A state park trails crew reported the collapse.

The Old Man is a natural rock formation that was created by a series of geologic events beginning an estimated 200 million years ago. Over time, nature carved out a 40-foot-tall profile resembling a gnarled human, and it soon became New Hampshire's most recognized symbol. The face appears on the state quarter, state highway signs and countless souvenirs and tourist brochures.

Millions of tourists have traveled through Franconia Notch to view the profile, 1,200 feet above Interstate 93 about 65 miles north of Concord. In the 19th century, the profile inspired New Hampshire statesman Daniel Webster to write: "In the mountains of New Hampshire, God Almighty has hung out a sign to show that there He makes men."

Dick Hamilton, president of White Mountain Attractions, a tourism group, has commuted through the notch every day for more than 30 years, and said goodnight to the Old Man every night when he drove by.

The night before the collapse was discovered, Hamilton, with his view blocked by the clouds, said, "Good night, boss, wherever you are."

"I've just lost my number one attraction," he said the next day.

 ©Teacher Created Resources, Inc.

Old Man of the Mountain Is Gone

Use information from the article on page 46 to answer the following questions:

1. How was New Hampshire's Old Man of the Mountain created? ______________________________
2. Why do you think the rock formation became New Hampshire's most recognizable symbol? ______________________________
3. How do you know that the craggy cliff face was in danger of falling for years? ______________________________
4. Referring to the Old Man, what does parks official Mike Pelchat mean when he says, "There's only so much you can do"? ______________________________
5. Which natural forces do Pelchat believe caused the collapse of the great mountainside landmark? ______________________________
6. Why are park officials not sure when the granite face actually fell? ______________________________
7. As New Hampshire's state symbol, where does the image of the Great Stone Face appear? ______________________________
8. Who was Daniel Webster? In his poetry, what did Webster say of the 40-foot profile of the old man's face? ______________________________
9. Now that the Old Man is no more, do you think tourists still will want to visit Franconia Notch? Explain. ______________________________
10. Do you think the jagged rock face should be rebuilt? Explain. ______________________________

Mirror Image

Discovered in 1805, the Old Man of the Mountain was a natural rock formation that resembled the profile of an old man's face. A series of five red granite ledges formed a heavy brow, large nose, pointy chin, and an unsmiling mouth. How would you describe your profile? You'll need two mirrors to view your face from the side. Which member of your family has a profile most like yours?

School Meals Getting Leaner

WASHINGTON, D.C. (AP) — School meals are getting leaner and more nutritious. Under pressure from federal officials, schools have trimmed fat, cholesterol and sodium from lunches and breakfasts and are offering children more fruits and vegetables, the government says.

A decade ago, barely a third of elementary schools offered students low-fat lunches. Now, four of every five schools do, according to an Agriculture Department report.

Schools have lowered the overall fat content of meals from 38 percent of calories to 34 percent of calories, the report said. Under USDA rules, the maximum is supposed to be 30 percent. Levels of saturated fat also are down.

"School meals reach nearly 27 million children each day, sometimes providing the most nutritious meal a child receives," said Agriculture Secretary Dan Glickman. "Fortunately, more than ever before, these meals are hitting the mark in providing good nutrition and healthy selections."

The report is based on a survey conducted during the 1998-99 school year and follows up a similar study done in 1991-92 that had alarmed federal officials. The Agriculture Department began requiring schools to meet minimum standards for nutrients and the 30 percent maximum for fat content.

Schools have altered their menus and food preparation. Now, turkey and chicken are substituted for beef to lower the fat content. Cafeteria workers skim fat from broth before making gravy. Schools offer a range of fresh fruits that are popular with kids, including strawberries, melons and even kiwis.

Over the objections of the beef industry, the government also has allowed schools to offer yogurt and soy products, such as veggie-burgers, as meat substitutes.

"What we've really been focusing on for the last six years is to enhance our school meals so that they do offer nutrient-dense foods that will benefit our children," said Marilyn Hurt, president of the American School Food Service Association.

But offering healthy meals is one thing; getting kids to eat them is another.

 ©Teacher Created Resources, Inc.

Schools Counting Calories

Use information from the article on page 48 to answer the following questions:

1. How many children eat school meals each day?____________________

2. Why are more and more schools offering students low-fat food? ____________________

3. According to the article, when was the most recent school food survey conducted? What U.S. government agency did the study? ____________________

4. In 1991, how many elementary schools offered students reduced-fat lunches?

5. Now, four out of five schools offer students leaner lunches. Is your school one of them? How do you know? ____________________

6. Schools have made food more nutritious by reducing the amounts of what three ingredients?

7. According to the Agriculture Department, what is the highest percent of calories that should come from fat?____________________

8. Are you concerned about the fat content of the food you eat? Why or why not?____________________

9. Give two examples of how schools have changed their food preparation in order to offer healthier selections.____________________

10. What is meant by the sentence, "But offering healthy meals is one thing; getting kids to eat them is another"? ____________________

What's for Lunch?

How do you think you'd do as a school lunch planner? Try putting together a week's worth of low-fat meals. For fun, complete your project by printing your menu on a piece of paper shaped like one of the fruits listed below. Will you offer peanut butter and jelly?

- banana
- orange
- pineapple
- pear
- strawberry
- watermelon

World's Smallest Lizard Discovered

BEATA ISLAND, Dominican Republic (AP) — Two American biologists have discovered the world's smallest known gecko—a lizard so tiny it can curl up comfortably on a dime.

The Jaragua gecko is the smallest of all 23,000 species of reptiles, birds, and mammals, researchers said.

Richard Thomas and Blair Hedges found the dark brown lizard on the Dominican Republic's remote Beata Island in 1998. Their findings appear in the *Caribbean Journal of Science.*

The Jaragua gecko measures only 1.6 centimeters—a sliver more than half an inch—from the base of its tail to its snout.

"We don't know if they get any smaller," said Thomas, of the University of Puerto Rico. "We suspect reptiles have a physiological limit and we are approaching that limit."

The geckos were found on a desert island also home to giant lizards known as rhinoceros iguana. The geckos are slightly smaller than a related species living several islands away in the British Virgin Islands.

Hedges, an associate professor at Penn State, speculates the gecko may have moved across a land bridge between the main island of Hispaniola and Beata Island during the last ice age.

The tiny lizard is one of about 80 species of Caribbean gecko, a family of soft-skinned, insect-eating lizards that have short, stout bodies and suction pads on their feet. It's unclear how many Jaragua geckos exist in the world.

The environment probably played a role in how the lizard became so small, Hedges said. Over millions of years, they likely filled a niche held in other places by small insect-eating spiders, he said.

The scientists believe the lizard eats tiny ants, spiders and soil-dwelling mites. Its size makes it vulnerable to tarantulas, snakes, centipedes and even other lizards.

The lizard, whose scientific name is *Sphaerodactylus ariasae*, was named after Yvonne Arias, a biologist and president of the Jaragua Group, a nonprofit organization that helps preserve the Dominican Republic's Jaragua National Park, which includes Beata Island.

Arias said the island's remoteness—it takes five hours by boat to reach Beata, a desolate isle of coral rock and limestone where about 70 fisherman are the only human inhabitants—probably has helped protect the habitat.

"Pressure from ecological groups has protected Beata Island up to now," she said on a recent expedition where she found one lizard under a coconut shell and the other in a pile of dry leaves. "But we need more resources to educate people and to protect it."

 ©Teacher Created Resources, Inc.

Island Lizard Tiniest Ever

Use information from the article on page 50 to answer the following questions:

1. Biologists Richard Thomas and Blair Hedges found the world's smallest lizard on Beata Island. Where is the island located? ______________________________

2. Why is Beata Island considered so remote (out of the way)? ______________________________

3. Why do you think Hedges can't prove that the sliver-sized reptile reached Beata Island by way of a land bridge? ______________________________

4. Other than under coconut shells or in piles of leaves, where else on the desolate isle might geckos be found? ______________________________

5. From snout to tail, what is the length of the tiny lizard? ______________________________

6. In addition to noting its size, how does the author of this story describe the appearance of the gecko? ______________________________

7. Name an object, other than a dime, that a Jaragua gecko could comfortably curl up on.
____

8. According to the American scientists, on what does the record-setting creature most likely feed?
____

9. What is the lizard's scientific name? After whom was it named? ______________________________

10. Why do you think researchers find it difficult to determine how many Jaragua geckos exist in the world? ______________________________

Small World

Did you know that the bee hummingbird is the smallest bird in the world? Look in an encyclopedia to find out the difference in size between this brightly-colored bird and the even smaller Jaragua gecko. How many species of hummingbirds are there? How did the tiny birds get their name? Can you name the smallest mammal in the world?

Museum Holds Show for Woodcarver

WASHINGTON, D.C. (AP) — The story goes that Olowe of Ise carved wood so skillfully that when the king summoned him to portray an important guest, the African sculptor could carve underneath his robe so the guest wasn't even aware he was a model.

"He was so good, he could do it by feel," said Roslyn A. Walker, curator of the first one-man show ever assembled for the prolific Nigerian artist.

She warns that no one knows if Olowe's carving-by-touch tale is exaggerated, but, "I think that's an extraordinary story."

Many African artists remain anonymous. Little is known about Olowe and the meanings of his unusual carvings because written records were scarce in that part of the world during his turn-of-the-century career carving intricate figures, columns and doors for African palaces.

The exhibit, at the National Museum of African Art, and an accompanying 150-page catalog of the show that Walker authored, was the first complete work on the artist.

Olowe of Ise (pronounced Oh-loh-way of EE-say), born about 1875, worked for kings of the Yoruba people, a group that lives predominantly in Nigeria.

Olowe began as a messenger in the king's court toward the end of the 1800s, and is believed to have died in 1938.

How he learned his art is not known, but a traditional song of praise, as recorded by his fourth wife, Oloju-ifun Olowe, calls him a strong and apparently dangerous man:

"He...carves the iroko tree with the ease of carving a calabash,

He who meets you unawares risks

Becoming a sacrificial victim.

Whoever meets you unawares

Sees trouble."

The iroko tree is know for its especially durable and parasite-resistant wood; a calabash is a gourd-like squash.

 ©Teacher Created Resources, Inc.

Woodcarver Gets One-Man Show

Use information from the article on page 52 to answer the following questions:

1. What kind of art did Olowe of Ise create? For whom did he work?
2. About how old was the sculptor when he began working as a messenger in the king's court?
3. How did Olowe of Ise learn to carve wood?
4. Do you believe that Olowe was able to sculpt "by feel"?
5. Why is it so hard to prove that the Yoruba artist could work on a piece of wood without looking at it?
6. Why might Olowe not want to tell a guest of the king that he was carving a figure of the visitor?
7. Name three kinds of work that the Nigerian sculptor produced for African palaces.
8. Explain how the words in the first line of the song of praise lead you to believe that the artist was strong.
9. Who put together the exhibit of the woodcarver's work? Where was it displayed?
10. Do you think that Olowe of Ise deserves a one-man show?

An Extraordinary Tale

Try using exaggeration to tell a story. Write an account of an unusual experience that could happen to you if you went to one of the places listed below. Make your story so incredible that it is hard to believe. How far can you stretch the truth?

- amusement park
- baseball stadium
- candy factory
- shopping mall
- toy store
- wax museum

They Creep and Crawl at Insectarium

PHILADELPHIA, Pa. (AP) — Five-year-old Andrew Belcher was about to eat a worm, but he dropped it on the floor before he could pop it in his mouth.

"You don't want to eat that!" Christi Cullen warned.

The young museum guide fished out a new cheese-covered worm and handed it to him.

"Tastes like a cheese doodle," Andrew said.

Cheese-covered meal worms are one of many treats awaiting brave-hearted, strong-stomached visitors to The Philadelphia Insectarium. If it creeps, crawls, stings or bites, you'll probably find it here.

Some of the specimens in the 6,000-square-foot museum are alive in natural habitats. The rest weren't so lucky—they're mounted on the walls.

Part zoo, part museum, the Insectarium has been delighting children and grossing out their parents since 1992. It's owned and operated by a man who has made a career of killing bugs: Steve Kanya of Steve's Bug-Off, an exterminating company housed in the same building.

Kanya opened his museum after he noticed children stopping to look at his catches of the day—a motley collection of rats, mice and insects he put in the window to attract business.

His museum workers are old bug hands.

"When I was young I was always the one out digging in the dirt and picking up worms and saying, 'Ooh! Look at this!'" Director Maureen Kennedy said.

The museum shows off insects from around the world, including bugs that look like ordinary tree leaves and insects so ornate that they are worn as living jewelry in Mexico.

Visitors are allowed to touch many of the dead bugs from Africa, Asia and Australia.

The star attraction is a most unpopular visitor—the American cockroach. In the museum's "Cockroach Kitchen," thousands live amid linoleum and wooden cabinets in a glass display case.

The museum aims to teach children that insects do more than sting, bite and annoy; they're a vital part of the ecosystem: termites dispose of fallen trees, millipedes stir up dirt to make room for the plants and bees and butterflies pollinate flowers.

"Without bugs, the world would be very different," Mrs. Kennedy said. "It'd be a lot dirtier, and probably not as pretty."

Bug-filled Museum

Use information from the article on page 54 to answer the following questions:

1. What is on display at The Philadelphia Insectarium? ______________________
2. Why do you think that the Insectarium is described as "part zoo, part museum"? ______________________
3. How did Steve Kanya get the idea of opening a museum filled with bugs? ______________________
4. How are dead insects exhibited in the 6,000 square foot space? ______________________
5. The museum features insects from around the world. Name two interesting facts about these specimens. ______________________
6. According to the story, which bugs are visitors allowed to touch? ______________________
7. Why do you think that "Cockroach Kitchen" is the most popular attraction at the Insectarium? ______________________
8. In what way do millipedes help the ecosystem (community of plants and animals)? ______________________
9. What does director Maureen Kennedy mean when she says that without bugs the world would "probably not (be) as pretty"? ______________________
10. Would you like to visit the Philadelphia Insectarium? Explain. ______________________

Pick-a-pet

The place in which an animal normally lives is called its habitat. Suppose that you wanted to keep one of the animals listed below as a pet. Design a natural habitat for the creature. Include things that the animal will need to survive. Does your pet eat bugs?

- fish
- hamster
- iguana
- snake
- turtle
- tarantula

Post-It Notes Turn 20

MAPLEWOOD, Minn. (AP) — They're not just canary yellow anymore, and they're not always square. Post-it Notes have come a long way in 20 years.

The little notes are now available in 56 shapes, 27 sizes and 50 colors. There also are Post-it Flags, Post-it Easel Pads, Post-it Pop-up Dispensers, Post-it Self-Stick Bulletin Boards and more.

The ubiquitous little bits of paper with sticky backing made by 3M Company turned 20 in 2000.

"My biggest reward as an inventor is to see so many people use and appreciate my product," said Art Fry, the 3M scientist who invented the Post-it Note.

It might never have happened if Fry hadn't been a singer in his church choir.

Fry would use slips of paper to mark his place in the hymnal, but they constantly fell out. He knew he needed a better way to keep his place or he'd forever be out of sync.

Then Fry heard about a unique adhesive Spencer Silver had developed in a 3M lab. It was sticky but could be repositioned. Fry knew he had the answer to his bookmark dilemma.

A short time later, Fry wrote a note on his bookmark and stuck it on a report going to one of his colleagues. Only then did he realize he had a new way to communicate and organize information.

After initial market tests in 1977 drew little interest, the Maplewood-based company decided to give away thousands of the little Post-it pads. Consumers overwhelmingly liked the idea.

3M began selling Post-it Notes in 1980. Two years later, the company introduced Post-it Printed Notes. In 1990 came the Post-it Pop-up Dispenser to keep the notes close at hand.

In 1996, the concept went digital with Post-it Software Notes. And 3M wasn't done yet. In 2000, the company introduced 4-inch-square lined Post-it Notes.

 ©Teacher Created Resources, Inc.

Post-it Notes: Still Going Strong

Use information from the article on page 56 to answer the following questions:

1. What are Post-it Notes? When did 3M Company begin selling them?
2. Why do you think that 3M decided to give away thousands of samples when the product was first introduced?
3. Describe the shape and color of the first sticky-note pads.
4. Before inventing the little notes, what dilemma did Art Fry have while singing in his church choir?
5. What was so special about the adhesive (glue) that Spencer Silver developed for 3M?
6. Name one problem Fry might have had if he used very sticky glue on the backs of the pieces of paper.
7. When did the 3M scientist realize that the bits of paper could be used for more than bookmarks?
8. Why do you think that the Maplewood-based company produces Post-it Notes in so many different sizes, shapes, and colors?
9. Why might a person buy a Post-it Pop-up Dispenser?
10. According to Fry, what is the best part of being the inventor of Post-it Notes?

Noteworthy

In 2000, 3M introduced 4-inch-square lined Post-it Notes. If you had a pad of these notes, how might the little slips of paper come in handy? Make a list of 10 ways you could use 3M's new product. Then ask two friends for their suggestions. Are their ideas the same as yours?

Stalagmites in Caves Show History

WASHINGTON, D.C. (AP) — Stalagmites created over thousands of years in New Mexico caves preserve a rainfall climate record of the arid Southwest and help explain why ancient Americans fled the high, dry mountains and settled in river valleys some 700 years ago, researchers say.

Victor J. Polyak of the University of New Mexico said that two-foot-long stalagmites taken from Carlsbad Caverns and from two other caves contain mineral deposition rings that correspond to levels of precipitation in the region.

Polyak, first author of a study in the journal *Science*, said the rings formed in the stone by the slow dripping of mineral-rich water are similar to growth rings found in tree trunks.

"We sliced the stalagmites and then made thin sections from the bottom to the top," said Polyak. Each section contained distinct bands of calcite deposition.

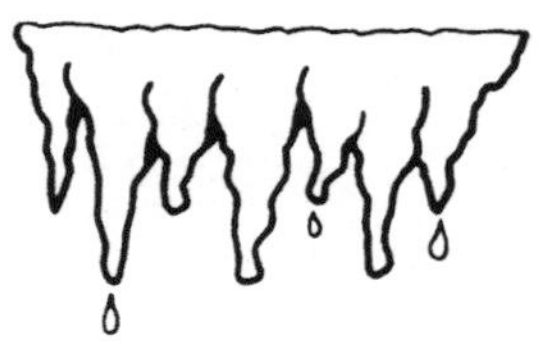

"The drier years will form thin bands (about .06 millimeter thick) and the wet years will form thicker bands (about .2 millimeter)," said Polyak. "During very dry seasons, the stalagmites stopped growing." The researchers found evidence for wet periods from about 4,000 years ago to about 800 years ago. They then compared this record with the known cultural history of the ancient Americans, such as the Pueblo, who lived in the Southwest.

"We found that the changes in the cultural history correspond to the climate changes," said Polyak. "The correlation seems consistent from 4,000 years ago to 700 years ago, when the stalagmites quit growing."

He said that the stalagmite growth apparently stopped at the beginning of a dry period that continues to this day. It was about 700 years ago that the Pueblo abandoned their mountain and high plateau villages and moved into river valleys.

Polyak said a wet period that started about 3,000 years ago roughly corresponds to an era when the ancient peoples settled and started raising maize or corn.

Stalagmite Rings Record Rainfall

Use information from the article on page 58 to answer the following questions:

1. Stalagmites are limestone columns shaped liked cones rising from the floor of a cave. How are they formed? ____

____

2. Where did researcher Victor J. Polyak get the two-foot-long stalagmites used in his study?

____

____

3. How did the New Mexico scientists cut up the stalagmites in order to study the bands of mineral deposits?____

____

4. When Polyak looks at the rings of calcite, what is he reminded of? ______________________

____

5. What caused the mineral deposition rings to vary in width? ______________________

____

6. If a calcite band measures .12 millimeter thick, was the ring formed during a dry or wet year? Explain. ____

____

7. Why do you think stalagmites stop growing during very dry seasons? ______________________

____

8. What fact from the story leads you to believe that New Mexico has remained a dry region for hundreds of years?____

____

9. Why do you think ancient Americans were so dependent upon rainfall?______________________

____

____

10. About 1,000 years ago, where did the Pueblo live? Where do they live now?______________________

____

____

Weather Wise

You don't have to slice open a stalagmite to find out about precipitation records in your area. Just locate the weather report in your local newspaper. Read the precipitation section to learn about record highs and lows. Would you consider this a dry year or a wet one for your region? Explain. For the record, what are stalactites?

Giant, Stinking Flower Blooms

LONDON, England (AP) — They held their breath for days, waiting for a gigantic flower to bloom for the fourth time this century. Then they held their noses.

But titan arum, which hadn't bloomed in London's Kew Gardens in 33 years, didn't live up to its reputation as a giant stinker.

"Disappointing," said Austin Hardy, 11, who came with five giggling friends wearing white face masks in anticipation of a major gross-out.

"I've got a very big nose and I couldn't smell anything," Monica Foster said.

Botanists and curiosity-seekers had been waiting since Monday for the 10-foot-tall plant to bloom, and the line of visitors stretched for 500 yards this afternoon.

Today's group was just too late, said Peter Boyce, a botanist at Kew.

Tuesday night, though, the bloom was something else, filling a Kew conservatory with its signature scent.

"It was quite overpowering at about 8 o'clock—a mixture of rotting flesh and burning sugar with ammonia over the top. It was a bit like a rubbish bin in summertime," Boyce said.

The smell—also described as fish-like—subsided within hours.

In the last few days the flower has been growing at an incredible rate—between four and six inches a day. Now its bell shape has fully opened to reveal a rich crimson color.

The titan arum, the largest flower in the world, has bloomed only four times at Kew Gardens, in 1889, 1901, 1926, and 1963.

Warned of the impending bloom, horticulturists and amateur gardeners hovered nearby and at last were rewarded.

Naturalist Sir David Attenborough said the stench wears off after a couple of days.

"The smell of rotting flesh is at its strongest when it first opens. After a couple of days it diminishes," said Attenborough, who once found one of the rare plants in the forests of Sumatra, Indonesia, where it is called "the corpse flower."

Attenborough said the aroma is produced to attract the attention of the sweat bee, an insect that lives in Sumatra's rain forests.

"Flowers aren't designed to smell nice for the benefit of humans," he said. "Some do because they are pollinated by honey bees; but bluebottles or blowflies will do the job just as well."

 ©Teacher Created Resources, Inc.

Flower Makes a Big Stink

Use information from the article on page 60 to answer the following questions:

1. What newsworthy event occurred in London's Kew Gardens? ______________________________
____
2. How tall is titan arum? Besides Kew Gardens, where else can it be found? ______________
____
____
3. When was the last time the giant flower bloomed? _________________________________
____
4. Why did Austin Hardy and his friends visit the botanical gardens wearing face masks?
____
____
5. How does botanist (a person who studies plants) Peter Boyce describe the scent of the rare plant?
____
____
6. Do you think that "the corpse flower" is a good name for the giant plant? Tell why or why not.
____
____
7. What insect is attracted to the stench (foul odor) of the bloom? _________________________
____
____
8. What happened to the huge, stinking plant a few days before its petals fully opened?
____
____
9. List two facts from the story that lead you to believe that the blossom is probably exceptionally beautiful. ____
____
10. If the flower has such an awful odor, why do you think so many people wanted to smell it?
____
____

More Sightseeing

If you were touring London, you'd probably want to visit the Tower of London. Lots of people line up to see the tower's armor collection, the crown jewels, and the prison exhibit. Which display do you think would be most worth the wait? Explain.

Dolphins Show Language-Like Learning

WASHINGTON, D.C. (AP) — Researchers eavesdropping on the underwater signals between dolphins found the mammals quickly learn and repeat intricate signals from their friends, an ability thought to be an important step toward evolving a language.

Analysis of more than 1,700 whistle signals exchanged among bottlenose dolphins swimming along the Moray Firth coast of Scotland showed the animals routinely responded to each other with matching signals, often echoing identical whistles within seconds of each other.

This trading of signals suggests the dolphins are capable of "vocal learning," a prerequisite for evolving a spoken language, according to researcher Vincent M. Janik. A report on his study appears in the journal *Science*.

Janik, a Scottish biologist now at the Woods Hole Oceanographic Institute in Massachusetts, said the signaling pattern of the dolphins is similar to what experts believe happened when ancient human beings first began organized speech.

Matching or labeling communication, he said in the study, "has been hypothesized to have been an important step in the evolution of human language."

Although birds, such as parrots, are well known for their ability to imitate sounds made by others, "bottlenose dolphins are the only nonhuman mammals in which matching interactions with learned signal types have been found."

Janik said that the dolphins apparently use the matching whistle patterns to address each other and that the sounds may play a role in signaling membership of a group.

Earlier studies have shown young dolphins adopt a signature whistle pattern, rather like a name, early in life. Janik's study showed the mammals may use these signature whistles as a way of addressing a specific animal who may be swimming many feet away.

"Janik provides important evidence that vocal labeling is used by wild dolphins for social communication," Peter L. Tyack, a Woods Hole researcher, said in a commentary in *Science*.

 ©Teacher Created Resources, Inc.

Dolphins Have a Language of Their Own

Use information from the article on page 62 to answer the following questions:

1. What have scientists learned from listening to underwater signals between dolphins?
2. Where did the dolphin research take place? How many whistle signals were studied?
3. About how long does it take for a bottlenose dolphin to imitate another dolphin's whistle?
4. Name an animal other than a dolphin that has the ability to imitate sounds.
5. Before ancient humans began organized speech, how did they communicate with each other?
6. What does biologist Vincent M. Janik mean when he says dolphins may be capable of "vocal learning"?
7. In earlier studies, Janik found that "young dolphins adopt a signature whistle pattern." What does this mean?
8. Why do the aquatic mammals use signature whistles?
9. Do you think dolphins are intelligent animals? Explain.
10. If you could meet Janik, what's the first question you would ask him about wild dolphins?

If Animals Could Talk . . .

If dolphins could talk, what do you think they'd say to each other about human beings? Imagine a conversation between two bottlenose dolphins. Give them names. Then write down your thoughts in the form of a dialogue between the two sea creatures. By the way, do you know how to whistle?

Scientist: Hominid Walked Upright

JOHANNESBURG, South Africa (AP) — Hand bones of what researchers believe is the oldest complete skeleton of a human ancestor show the creature walked upright and also climbed trees, his discoverer says.

The find would appear to support the contention that human ancestors from the period lived both on the ground and in trees but did not swing from trees or walk on knuckles, the subject of debate among scientists.

British paleoanthropologist Ron Clarke, who announced the existence of the 3.3-million-year-old skeleton, has slowly been uncovering the remains. They are embedded in rock in Sterkfontein, a former lime quarry cave near Johannesburg that has yielded a number of hominid skulls since the 1930s.

The skull, leg bones and foot and ankle fragments were uncovered earlier. Clarke announced the left arm and hand had been found stretched out over where the head would have been.

Clarke is affiliated with the Johann Wolfgang Gothe University in Frankfurt, Germany. In an interview with Associated Press Television News, he said the 4-foot-tall creature's fingers were found clenched over the thumb.

He and fellow researchers have said they believe the ape man, scientifically known as *Australopithecus africanus,* fell down a 45-foot shaft.

"It was as though the fingers had curled as the individual was dying," he said. "What the hand tells us is that it was not a specialized hand like that of the apes. In other words, the fingers were not elongated for suspension from trees or for knuckle-walking on the ground."

The fingers were curved and the thumb was more powerful than that of a modern man, Clarke said, and thus still suitable for grasping tree branches.

Human ancestors like "Little Foot," as the media have named Clarke's Sterkfontein find, developed after an evolutionary split with the ancestors of apes. Paleontologists are divided over whether such ancestors lived only on the ground or also climbed trees like some primates.

Hand Bones Clue to Ape Man's Past

Use information from the article on page 64 to answer the following questions:

1. What did British paleoanthropologist Ron Clarke find in a cave near Johannesburg? ____________
2. How tall was the hominid? What is his scientific name? ____________
3. Where did the creature make his home? ____________
4. According to researchers, how did the ape man die? ____________
5. Besides "Little Foot's" left arm and hand, what other remains of the ape man have been found in Sterkfontein? ____________
6. What part of the 3.3-million-year-old skeleton led Clarke to believe that human ancestors walked upright? ____________
7. What does Clarke mean when he says that the creature's hand "was not a specialized hand like that of the apes"? ____________
8. How do the skeleton's fingers differ from those of a modern man? ____________
9. Why do you think the media (news organizations) named Clarke's find "Little Foot"? ____________
10. Would you like to help Clarke uncover the bones of the oldest complete skeleton of a human ancestor? Explain. ____________

Skeleton Key

The human skeleton consists of 206 bones. Look in an encyclopedia to find a picture of the bones in a human body. Then cut out a full-length picture of person from a newspaper or magazine. Label the picture to show the location of the bones listed below. By the way, where's your funny bone?

- clavicle
- sternum
- mandible
- tibia
- patella
- humerus

Study Suggests Orangutans Are Cultured

WASHINGTON, D.C. (AP) — Some orangutan parents teach their offspring to use leaves as napkins. Others say goodnight with a sputtering, juicy raspberry. And still others get water from a hole by dipping a branch and then licking the leaves.

These examples, researchers say, prove the orangutan is a cultured ape, able to learn new living habits and to pass them along to the next generation.

The discovery suggests that early primates may have developed the ability to invent new behaviors, such as tool use, as early as 14 million years ago.

"If the orangutans have culture, then it tells us that the capacity to develop culture is very ancient," says Birute Galdikas, a co-author of the study. In the march of evolution, "orangutans separated from our ancestors and from the African apes many millions of years ago," she said. The study suggests they may have had culture before they separated.

And though it is crude by human standards, orangutan culture is practiced independently by different groups and succeeding generations in the same way that human societies develop and perpetuate unique forms of music, architecture, language, clothing and art.

Galdikas and eight other scientists analyzed years of observations of the Southeastern Asian orangutan. They concluded that the ape has the ability to adopt and pass along learned behaviors.

For instance, members of bands in Borneo and Sumatra make a kiss-squeak noise by compressing the lips and drawing in air. Both groups used leaves to amplify the noise, but only members of the Borneo groups had discovered they could change the sound by cupping the hands over the mouth. The sounds are apparently used for communicating socially.

The opposite of the kiss-squeak is the raspberry—breath is blown out through compressed lips to make a splattering sound. Only one of the six groups does this habitually, and it seems to be related to a bedtime ritual, Galdikas said.

A group in Sumatra has learned to use leaves as gloves when handling spiny fruits. A second Sumatran band has learned to drink by dipping a leafy branch into a water-filled tree hole and then licking the moisture from the leaves. Galdikas said a group in Borneo routinely will force a small tree to the ground, riding it as it falls, and then grab nearby forest limbs before crashing to the ground.

Altogether, the researchers found 24 examples of behaviors that are routinely practiced by at least one group and passed to new generations.

 ©Teacher Created Resources, Inc.

Orangutans Lead a Cultured Life

Use information from the article on page 66 to answer the following questions:

1. Using information from paragraph two, define the word *culture*. ______
2. When do scientists at the Orangutan Foundation International believe primates first developed culture? ______
3. How many researchers analyzed the results of years of observations of apes in Borneo and Sumatra? ______
4. After completing their study, what did scientists conclude about the shy Southeast Asian orangutan? ______
5. What evidence is there that orangutans had culture before they separated from the African apes millions of years ago? ______
6. List five routine behaviors orangutans have invented. ______
7. Why is the raspberry described as the opposite of the kiss-squeak? ______
8. How do you think members of the Borneo group discovered a way to change the sound of a kiss-squeak? ______
9. What types of cultural "trademarks" do human societies develop and pass along to future generations? ______
10. Which one of the orangutan's learned habits do you think is most like human behavior? Which is the most unusual? ______

Traditional Values

Family traditions, like culture, are customs or beliefs that have been passed down from one generation to the next. Interview a parent to find out which behaviors routinely practiced by your family were learned from past generations. Which of those social skills or habits have your parents taught you? By the way, can you make a kiss-squeak or a raspberry noise?

Cave Dwellers Made Sandals

WASHINGTON, D.C. (AP) — There were no spiked heels, wing tips or cross trainers. But footwear crafted by American cave dwellers thousands of years ago was fashionable, though, and well-made.

"My guess is that these shoes were very stylish for the time," said Michael J. O'Brien, an anthropologist who analyzed 35 specimens of sandals, moccasins and slip-ons unearthed in a Missouri cave that was a popular campsite some 9,000 years ago.

The shoes were also very durable, he said. Of 35 samples recovered, 20 were compete or nearly complete. This enabled O'Brien and co-researcher from Louisiana State University to analyze and date the footgear for the first time, he said. A report on the study was published in the journal *Science*.

The oldest specimen was a sandal made from a woven, fibrous material that dated from about 9,400 years before the present. The most recent, about 1,000 years old, was a classic deerskin moccasin, probably made for a child.

Only the moccasins were made of leather, and the researcher said it is likely that the cave dwellers did not use leather for shoes much earlier than that.

All of the other shoes were made with fibrous plants that could be woven into a tough fabric used for the top, bottom and sides of the footwear. O'Brien said the most common material was from a yucca-like plant called rattlesnake master. The leaves were dried and plaited into cording that was then woven.

Footwear got hard use among the prehistoric Americans. The people, who have not been named, had to walk most places, since there were no horses. They had to hunt or gather all of their food and to haul water back to the cave, all jobs that took much walking.

Foot size, he said, appears to be much like that of modern humans. There is no way to tell if wearers of the ancient shoes were male or female, but the average length was about 10 ½ inches. O'Brien said this is about 8 ½ in modern American women's sizes.

"That suggests that these people fell within the size range of people today," he said.

The cave, which is in a bluff not far from the Missouri River, was a spectacular home, by the standards of the time.

"The cave is so dry and has been for the last 10,000 years that all this stuff was preserved," he said.

The shoes and other artifacts were unearthed some 40 years ago from cave deposits. Only recently, however, have researchers been able to precisely date each of the footwear specimens.

 ©Teacher Created Resources, Inc.

Old Shoes Found in Cave

Use information from the article on page 68 to answer the following questions:

1. What does Michael J. O'Brien do for a living? ______________________________
2. What artifacts (manmade objects) has O'Brien recently studied and dated? ______________________________
3. Where were the ancient shoes discovered? How long ago were they unearthed (dug up)? ______________________________
4. Which words in the first paragraph describe the cave dweller's shoes? ______________________________
5. How old is the deerskin moccasin? Who probably wore the ancient shoe? ______________________________
6. How were fibrous plants used to make sturdy (strong) sandals? ______________________________
7. Why did American cave dwellers need durable footgear? ______________________________
8. Why do you think that researchers are unable to tell whether the shoes were worn by males or females? ______________________________
9. If the cave had been damp, what might have happened to the old footwear? ______________________________
10. Why do you think that spiked heels were not crafted (made) by cave dwellers thousands of years ago? ______________________________

Shoe Business

Six kinds of shoes are mentioned in the article. Find the style names and circle them. Then, for the next week, scan your local newspaper for pictures of each type of footwear. How many can you find? Do you own a pair of cross trainers?

Scientists Solve Noisy Shrimp Puzzle

WASHINGTON, D.C. (AP) — Like a chorus of chattering castanets, the underwater drone of thousands of snapping shrimp can be so intense that submarines use the cacophony to hide from sonar.

But how do marine animals so small make a racket so large? Scientists have long been puzzled, but a group of European researchers has found the answer: the shrimp make bubbles that collapse with a pop powerful enough to kill small prey.

Snapping shrimp are 2-inch-long creatures equipped with a small claw and a huge, outsized claw, almost half the animal's length. The shrimp prowl the shallow waters of tropical seas with the big claw cocked, ready to seize a meal.

When the big claw closes at lightning speed, there is a sharp clicking sound. If there are enough shrimp in a school, the sound becomes rather like that of the crackling of burning dry twigs.

Clusters of tens of thousands of shrimp can make enough noise "to disturb underwater communications," according to Detlef Lohse, a physicist at the University of Twente in the Netherlands. "Submarines have used colonies of these shrimp to hide in the offshore waters of the United States."

The European researchers discovered the snapping shrimp secret when they put some of the creatures in a water tank equipped with ultra-high-speed cameras.

"We tickled them to make them close their claws," Lohse said.

He said the photos show that when the shrimp closes its claw very rapidly, it creates a high-speed water jet, moving at almost 70 miles per hour. The jet causes a sharp and brief drop in water pressure and instantly a bubble is formed and collapsed.

"A microscopic bubble grows to about 4 millimeters [a little more than an eighth of an inch]," Lohse said.

"When the pressure returns to normal, the bubble collapses and that makes the sound."

The time between the claw closure and the collapse of the bubble is 700 microseconds, he said. A microsecond is one-millionth of a second.

Collapse of the bubble also sends out a shock wave that, on a very small scale, is very powerful, he said.

The shock wave created by the snapping shrimp is not that powerful, Lohse said, but it is enough to provide the shrimp with a meal. The animal uses the shock wave to stun worms and other prey, he said.

 ©Teacher Created Resources, Inc.

Secret of the Snapping Shrimp

Use information from the article on page 70 to answer the following questions:

1. Why have snapping shrimp puzzled scientists for so long? ______________________________

   ____

2. Which sentence in the story describes the body and claws of the noisy marine animals?

   ____

   ____

3. Who found the answer to the snapping shrimp mystery? ______________________________

   ____

4. How do you think scientists "tickled" the small sea creatures in order to get them to make noise?

   ____

   ____

5. Why do you think researchers attached high-speed cameras to an experimental water tank?

   ____

   ____

6. Photos reveal that bubbles are formed when the shrimp closes its claw quickly. How does this happen? ______________________________

   ____

7. How big is the snapping shrimp's bubble? How long does it last before it collapses?

   ____

8. What two things occur when the bubble caves in? ______________________________

   ____

9. How does the shrimp capture its prey? ______________________________

   ____

10. Why is it so difficult for sonar to locate submarines that hide among schools of these shrimp?

    ____

    ____

What a Racket!

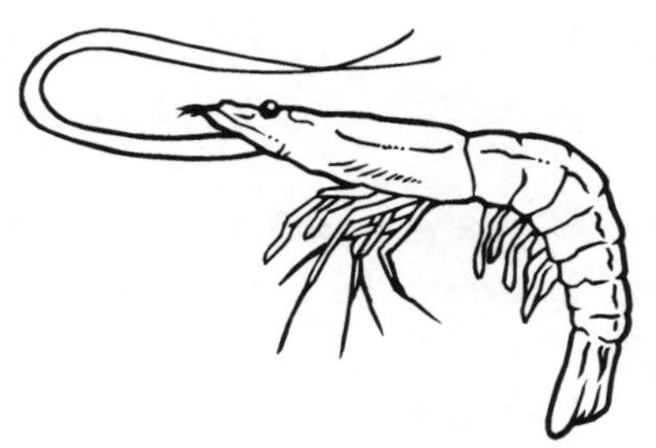

The author of this story uses many different words to tell about the sound made by shrimp. Scan the article to find five or more words that describe the racket. Then, using those words, make up a short story about a noisy situation. Will you write about "clattering castanets"?

Multiple Choice

General Directions

Use facts from the articles to complete the statements. Circle the letter of the correct answer, or record your answers on the "Multiple Choice Worksheet" (page 73).

Suggested Directions to the Student

1. Read the headline to get a clue about the topic of the story.
2. Number the paragraphs. Whenever possible, find paragraph proof for your answers.
3. Read the *entire* story before completing the statements.
4. Use the context of the article to figure out the meaning of unfamiliar words.
5. All true statements are based on the story. No additional information is needed to complete the sentences.
6. Statements can be completed out of order. The facts are not presented in the same order they are found in the article. (Ask, "Where in the article was the author looking when she wrote this statement?")
7. Along with the letter of the correct choice, either record the ending that makes a true statement or write a sentence that begins with the stem and ends with the correct choice.
8. Only one ending is true according to the article. Therefore, there are always two false or incorrect choices for each sentence completion.
9. Correct answers restate information found in the article using different words to express an idea but still keeping the choice "true."
10. Each of the false choices uses information from the article in an incorrect way. So, be sure to reread parts of the article to compare and contrast facts.
11. For statements where you have to infer meaning, pick the choice that makes the most sense according to the article.
12. If you are not sure of an answer, eliminate a choice that you know is incorrect. Then choose between the two choices that are left.
13. Use the supplemental activity to expand upon ideas presented in the article.

Multiple Choice Worksheet

Student Name: ______________________________ **Date:** ______________

Column Title: ______________________________

Paragraph Proof	Letter Answer	New Sentence
1.		
2.		
3.		
4.		
5.		
6.		
7.		
8.		
9.		
10.		

Score Box [ ]

Miniature Book Auction Scheduled

LONDON, England (AP) — A Bible the width of a thumbtack head is the smallest item up for sale in a rare auction of over 4,000 miniature books.

The smallest of the small, measuring 3/16 inch in height and width, is an Old Testament in German. The printed words are so small they appear as dots until read with a magnifying glass.

"We are still investigating when it was published but probably it is late 19th or early 20th century," said Mark Ghahramani of Christie's auction house.

The tiny tome is expected to sell for $800 to $1,280 in London.

"Book auctions sometimes include a few miniatures but a sale devoted to them is unusual and we have not had one since 1979," Ghahramani said.

The 4,000 little books dating from the 16th century to the 1990s were collected by Irene Winterstein, who was born in 1925. She kept them in display cabinets at her home in Zurich, Switzerland.

When she was 15 she bought a 1-inch by 2-inch black notebook to use as a diary. She was so fascinated that it led to a lifelong pursuit of miniature printed books.

During the Cold War, she found rare ones in Eastern Europe and would buy them with desired commodities like coffee and bed linen when foreign currency was unacceptable.

The Winterstein collection became internationally known and was examined by experts and collectors worldwide. It is being sold by her sons and is expected to bring in at least $320,000.

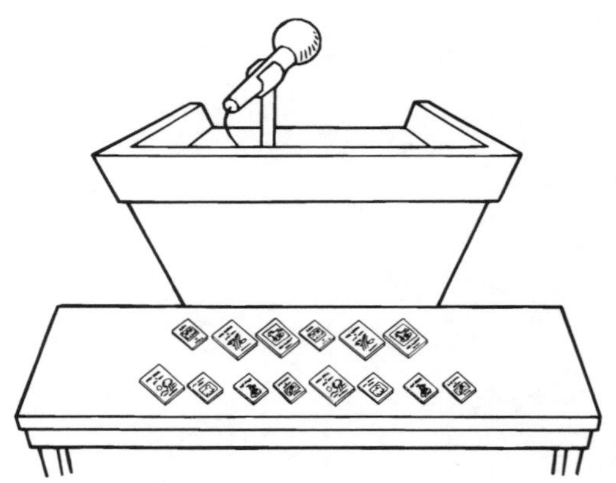

Tiny Books for Sale

Use facts from the article to complete each of the following statements:

1. You can guess that at auctions, an item is sold to the person who . . .
   a. offers to pay the highest price.
   b. makes the most money.
   c. is the oldest.
2. Christie's auction house . . .
   a. put 4,000 miniature (small) books up for sale.
   b. gave away a set of Bibles.
   c. opened an office in London.
3. Mark Ghahramani says miniature auctions . . .
   a. take place at least once a year.
   b. are very unusual.
   c. were first held in 1979.
4. Irene Winterstein became interested in tiny books when she . . .
   a. visited Eastern Europe.
   b. was 15 years old.
   c. bought a 12-inch notebook.
5. Winterstein bought some of the rare books . . .
   a. with coffee and bed linen.
   b. in the 16th century.
   c. Both *a* and *b* are correct.
6. The smallest item in Winterstein's collection . . .
   a. is shaped like a thumbnail.
   b. disappeared a year ago.
   c. measures 3/16 inch in height.
7. According to the story, the tiny Old Testament in German . . .
   a. has never been read.
   b. is really just a bunch of dots.
   c. will probably sell for about $1,000.
8. The long-time collector . . .
   a. displayed her books in cabinets.
   b. kept her little treasures out of sight.
   c. lived in a 400-year -old house.
9. Buyers from around the world are expected to . . .
   a. ask Winterstein's sons to stop the sale.
   b. pay more than $320,000 for the tomes (books).
   c. offer the most money for the diary.
10. People probably want to own miniature volumes because . . .
    a. they like to read with a magnifying glass.
    b. complete sets were published in Switzerland.
    c. tiny printed books are so rare.

Diminutive Diary

Irene Winterstein kept a diary in a small, black notebook. Find out why the tiny book fascinated her. Cut out seven pieces of paper, each 1" by 2" in size. Staple them together. Now, for the next week, write a diary entry on each of the little pages. Choose your words carefully—there's not much room!

L.A. Second-Grader Petitions School

LOS ANGELES, Calif. (AP) — When access to the monkey bars at Calvert Elementary School was restricted, 7-year-old Isabelle Glen-Lambert swung into action.

The second-grader went on the offensive when a rules change required students to earn tickets through good behavior in order to use the playground equipment.

"I didn't get real upset about it until I started talking it out with my friends," she said. "It wasn't fair that you had to get those dumb tags."

Principal Shelley Rivlin-Hollis said she decided on the change because children were getting hurt under the old system, which allowed an entire grade level at a time on the apparatus.

However, the decision was made without consulting the students.

So Isabelle—the granddaughter of a teachers' union lobbyist—collected several signatures (that of 5-year-old sister Rosie topped the list) and marched into the principal's office and asked for the old system.

"I wanted to give her the biggest hug," Rivlin-Hollis said. "It indicated she had a real sense of security here, and also that has she had an understanding of the democratic process."

Rivlin-Hollis turned the issue over to the student council. Representatives from grades three to five interviewed students, teachers and yard monitors to prepare. A debate was held.

In the end, a close vote overturned the rule and supported Isabelle's petition, but with a new proviso: only one classroom at a time will be allowed on the equipment.

Although pleased with the outcome, Isabelle said she did it because playground rights were at stake, not because she is gearing up for a political career. The little girl who has roamed the halls of the state capitol with her grandfather wants to be a singer.

"Would I like to be a lobbyist? No," she said. "When I went up to Sacramento, it seemed like a lot of work."

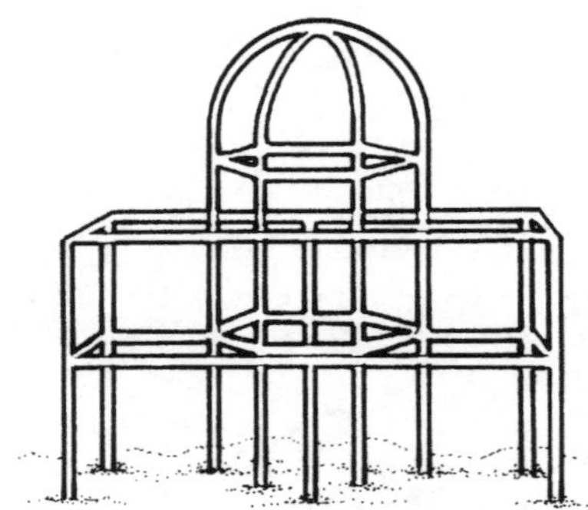

 ©Teacher Created Resources, Inc.

Playground Rights Upheld

Use facts from the article to complete each of the following statements:

1. Isabelle Glen-Lambert wanted to . . .
   a. change her school's playground rules. b. join the student council. c. put monkeys behind bars.
2. Calvert Elementary School Principal Shelly Rivlin-Hollis made up a new set of playground rules . . .
   a. in order to prevent accidents. b. without asking the students for advice. c. Both *a* and *b* are correct.
3. According to the new rules, students had to . . .
   a. earn the right to use the playground. b. sign up to use the swing. c. repair the broken apparatus (equipment).
4. Under the old rules, too many children . . .
   a. argued with the yard monitors. b. ended up in the principal's office. c. used the play area at the same time.
5. The story suggests that Rivlin-Hollis was . . .
   a. impressed with the little girl's efforts. b. looking forward to meeting the child's relatives. c. unhappy with Isabelle's behavior.
6. To help solve the playground problem, the student council . . .
   a. held a debate at the state Capitol. b. talked with the students and staff. c. had everyone sign another petition.
7. After the question of playground use was put to a vote . . .
   a. students weren't allowed in the play area. b. Isabelle was pleased with the results. c. only one classroom had permission to use the yard.
8. In the end, children no longer had to . . .
   a. get tags to enjoy the playground. b. worry about ever getting hurt. c. behave properly in school.
9. You can guess that a lobbyist tries to . . .
   a. spend time talking with youngsters. b. work in fancy hotels. c. get lawmakers to favor some special interest.
10. The seven-year-old girl took action because she . . .
    a. didn't want to disobey her grandfather. b. wanted to become a politician. c. thought her classmates were being treated unfairly.

Play by the Rules

Imagine that your school's principal held a playground-safety poster contest. Design a sign that includes a set of safety rules and a picture. Make the rules easy to understand. Will you allow students to swing from the monkey bars?

Blast Rocketed Pieces of Mars Down to Earth

WASHINGTON, D.C. (AP) — A massive explosion on Mars millions of years ago blasted rocks into orbit and some of that material landed on Earth, researchers say.

Kurt Marti, a planetary chemist at the University of California at San Diego, said that a 40-pound meteorite that landed in Africa in 1962 has been identified as a bit of Mars.

The meteorite was observed as it crashed to Earth in Nigeria and was quickly recovered. It is named Zagami for the region where it hit.

A study of the chemistry of Zagami was published in the journal *Science*.

Marti, the study's lead author, said that gas trapped in bubbles within glass inside the meteorite has been chemically matched with the atmospheric composition found on Mars by the *Viking* spacecraft.

Another meteorite, found in Antarctica and analyzed in 1985, also had the chemical signature of the Martian atmosphere, said Marti. A third meteorite may have the same characteristics, he said.

Marti said Zagami was wandering in space for about three million years before it landed on Earth. According to him, it's not known where Zagami originated on Mars, but there are lots of candidate sites.

"Mars is filled with craters created by collisions," he said. Astronomers are now searching Mars by telescope to find sites with minerals like those in the Zagami meteorite.

Marti said it is assumed that the explosion that ejected Zagami was caused by a large asteroid or comet slamming into Mars. "It would require a very major collision," he said, "It is a very rare event."

Heat created by the collision melted rock that cooled quickly into glass, he said, and some of the Martian atmosphere was trapped and formed bubbles within the glass. It is this gas that has been compared with the chemistry found in the Martian atmosphere by the *Viking* landers in 1976.

 ©Teacher Created Resources, Inc.

Meteorite from Mars

Use facts from the article to complete each of the following statements:

1. An explosion on Mars millions of years ago caused . . .
   a. rocks to be blasted into space. b. chemical changes on Earth. c. many problems for scientists.

2. Rocks from Mars have . . .
   a. damaged spacecraft. b. landed on Earth. c. been found by Kurt Marti.

3. Meteorites, or chunks of matter, from Mars have landed in . . .
   a. Nigeria. b. Antarctica. c. Both *a* and *b* are correct.

4. The meteorite that landed in Africa . . .
   a. weighed 32 pounds. b. was named Zagami. c. was not discovered for a long time.

5. According to the article, the name "Zagami" refers to . . .
   a. an African author. b. a scientific journal. c. a place in Nigeria.

6. Scientists study the chemistry of meteorites to find out . . .
   a. where other rocks have landed. b. what the rocks are made of. c. when the next planet explosion will occur in space.

7. Kurt Marti, a planetary chemist, reported that the gas trapped inside Zagami . . .
   a. matches the Martian atmosphere. b. can be seen with special glasses. c. is impossible to study.

8. Marti believes an explosion took place on Mars . . .
   a. after the *Viking* spacecraft landed. b. when a comet or asteroid hit the planet. c. about 40 years ago.

9. Glass formed inside the meteorite when . . .
   a. the rock landed on Earth. b. chemists heated the rock. c. Martian rock melted and then cooled quickly.

10. The collision, or crash, that occurred on Mars . . .
    a. takes place only once every 30 years. b. is a very unusual event. c. was caused by cosmic rays.

Student Stumbles Upon Rock

Some meteorites are tiny; others weigh as much as 60 tons. Pretend that you found a meteorite. Write a story about your discovery. Tell how, when, and where you found the rock. Include a description or picture of your souvenir from space.

Fiddleheads Can Mean Big Business

BOLTON, Vt. (AP) — Fourteen-year-old Ashley Stevens fell out of his canoe into the frigid Winooski River, climbed onto the muddy bank and picked fiddleheads for five hours as his wet clothes stiffened and dried in the frosty spring air.

It was worth it. On that early May day, Ashley made $50 for the 86 pounds of ferns he hauled in to the weigh station.

And he's made about that much every day of the fiddlehead season.

"I know where to go," said Ashley, who grew up along the Winooski.

For four or five weeks a year in Vermont, fiddleheads, young ferns found near water in the Northeast, are big business for anyone who cares to pick them. Before they uncurl to their mature height, the plants resemble violin heads.

The ferns, which taste like asparagus when cooked, are usually sauteed in butter or olive oil and served as a side dish. Restaurants offer them as a seasonal specialty; supermarkets sell them by the pound.

John Farrar, the fiddlehead maestro of Richmond, parks his pickup every evening and waits for the pickers to bring their mesh bags of fiddleheads for weighing. Farrar often collects more than 1,000 pounds of the tightly-curled green discs.

He drives them to W.S. Wells and Son in Wilton, Maine, where they are prepared for sale fresh, in cans, and dried in soup mix. Wells processes about 35 tons a year, all from local pickers who bring in the fiddleheads by bag or bucket.

Farrar is careful to take only ostrich ferns. Some other kinds are said to cause cancer in cows or stomach upset in humans.

"They all kind of look like fiddleheads," said Butch Wells, owner of W.S. Wells and Son. "I've had people drive for two hours with 200 pounds of the wrong kind of fiddleheads."

He said he believed he was having some fiddleheads for supper that night. "I've had them in stews, and I've had them in quiche, and something they call Impossible Pie. And we just have them plain, as a side dish."

Even his kids eat fiddleheads.

"They like pickled fiddleheads," Wells said. "They don't like them any other way."

 ©Teacher Created Resources, Inc.

Fiddleheads for Sale

Use facts from the article to complete each of the following statements:

1. Fiddleheads are . . .
   a. musical instruments. b. young ferns. c. pickup trucks.

2. The young plants look like . . .
   a. phonograph discs. b. bunches of asparagus. c. violin heads.

3. The ferns must be gathered when they are young because when the plants mature they . . .
   a. lose their green color. b. uncurl. c. weigh close to 200 pounds.

4. The tightly-curled discs . . .
   a. grow in the northeastern United States. b. are picked 45 weeks a year. c. Both *a* and *b* are correct.

5. People who harvest fiddleheads . . .
   a. sell the ferns for a good price. b. look for the plants all year round. c. are usually able to cook side dishes.

6. After Ashley Stevens fell into the Winooski River, he probably didn't bother to change his clothes because he . . .
   a. was going for a swim in a few hours. b. wanted to spend all of his time gathering ferns. c. needed to keep an eye on his canoe.

7. W.S. Wells and Son in Wilton, Maine, . . .
   a. puts frozen fiddleheads in bags and buckets. b. gets the plants ready for sale. c. makes 35 tons of soup mix.

8. Butch Wells points out that ostrich ferns . . .
   a. often cause stomach problems. b. cost more than other types of curly plants. c. are the only kind of fiddleheads that he sells.

9. Freshly picked fiddleheads . . .
   a. can be found in supermarkets. b. cost about $50 a pound. c. must be eaten within five hours.

10. According to the article, the coiled leaves . . .
    a. taste awful if eaten plain. b. can be pickled. c. should never be put in a pie.

Fiddle Fun

A fiddlehead is a young fern that resembles the head of a violin, or fiddle. But do you know the meaning of "fiddle-faddle," "fiddle-de-dee," "fiddlestick," and "fiddlesticks"? Look in a dictionary to find out which words mean the same thing. Which word names an object used to play a violin?

Parents Can Use Allowances To Teach

NEW YORK, N.Y. (AP) — Children's book writer Amy Nathan knows that giving a kid an allowance doesn't always produce the intended results.

When one of her sons was young, she was looking for a way to get him to make his bed and clean his room. She offered him an allowance with a "bonus" when his room was tidy and a "penalty" when it wasn't.

"But he wasn't interested yet in money," Nathan said. "There wasn't anything he really wanted to buy, so he didn't really need an allowance." And, of course, his bed went unmade.

That said, allowances—when kids are ready for them—can be useful tools for teaching them how to manage money and, if tied to chores, how to earn it.

Surveys by *Zillions*, the children's online magazine published by *Consumer Reports*, have found that more than half of American kids get an allowance. Most get their first allowances between ages 7 and 11.

Nearly all children who get allowances have assigned chores, with 70 percent saying that cleaning their room is a requirement for collecting their cash each week. About 25 percent must put some of their money into savings.

How much kids get varies greatly. One formula sets the weekly rate at 50 cents for each year of a child's age, meaning a 7-year-old would get $3.50 a week. Others get $1 a week for each year.

And that's generally just the "base pay," according to the allowance data collected by the Web site *www.kidsmoney.org.* Some kids get bonuses for special chores, like helping with yard work. Others get annual cost-of-living increases. Still others get more cash if their grades in school improve.

Nathan, who wrote *The Kids' Allowance Book*, is a firm believer in giving kids allowances, despite the fact that her son initially didn't respond to cash incentives to clean his room.

"You need to wait until you feel your kid is interested in money and knows what it can do," Nathan said. "Then you really can use allowances to help kids learn how to manage money."

To teach young children the concept of budgeting, Nathan likes what she calls the "jar system"—a series of jars marked for different things such as spending, saving, holiday gifts, music, church or charity. "If you give them their allowances in coins, it's easier for them to divide it up," she said.

 ©Teacher Created Resources, Inc.

Kids Learn to Manage Money

Use facts from the article to complete each of the following statements:

1. Amy Nathan wrote a book about . . .
   a. her youngest son. b. the benefits of allowance. c. easy ways to make a bed.
2. In *The Kids' Allowance Book*, Nathan explains how . . .
   a. the Internet works. b. to get children to read. c. youngsters learn to manage money.
3. The children's book writer discovered . . .
   a. her son always keeps his room tidy. b. boys are constantly buying things. c. not all kids want their own money.
4. A young child may not be interested in getting an allowance because . . .
   a. no one in his family needs cash. b. he doesn't understand yet how money works. c. his parents get everything they need for free.
5. Surveys by *Zillions* found that most American children . . .
   a. complain about having to save. b. get their first allowance by age 12. c. don't like to spend money.
6. The publication reports that the amount of a youngster's allowance is often . . .
   a. based on a child's age. b. determined by a secret formula. c. the same for everyone.
7. Parents often pay their children for . . .
   a. getting good grades in school. b. helping out at home. c. Both *a* and *b* are correct.
8. Seventy percent of children who get weekly "pay" have to . . .
   a. keep their rooms clean. b. collect the trash. c. put 25 percent of their money into savings.
9. Some parents give bonuses to children who . . .
   a. can figure out the cost of living. b. do special jobs. c. admit that yard work is a chore.
10. The "jar system" helps young children to . . .
    a. pick out the best holiday gifts. b. stop worrying about. the need to save. c. decide how to spend their cash wisely.

Moneywise

How do your opinions about money compare with those of other kids? Find out by going to *www.zillions.org* and clicking on "Money Smarts" and then on "Money Q&A." Next, click on a topic that interests you and see what kids had to say. Which suggestions do you agree with? Which do you disagree with? Can you offer another solution to the problem?

Rare U.S. Gold Coin Fetches $7.59M

NEW YORK, N.Y. (AP) — A gold coin that never had a chance to be spent has proved to be worth a lot more than its $20 face value.

The 1933 Double Eagle was sold at the Sotheby's auction house for $7.59 million.

"It is now, as of this evening, the most valuable coin in the world," said Henrietta Holsman Fore, director of the U.S. Mint.

The coin, which had vanished for decades until undercover Secret Service agents recovered it, was sold by the government to an anonymous bidder.

The Mint had estimated the coin's value at $4 million to $6 million.

Thousands of Double Eagles were minted in 1933 but were not circulated because President Franklin D. Roosevelt took the nation off the gold standard.

The 1933 Double Eagles, featuring a standing Liberty on one side and an eagle on the reverse, were ordered melted down in 1937. Two were given to the Smithsonian Institution and several others vanished—stolen in an inside job, according to the Mint.

The theft wasn't discovered until 1944, according to the Mint. Nine coins were recovered, but one—still considered stolen property—ended up in the collection of Egypt's King Farouk.

The coin disappeared in the 1950s and surfaced again in 1996 when British coin dealer Stephen Fenton tried selling it to undercover Secret Service agents in New York. An out-of-court settlement with Fenton cleared the way for the auction, the Mint said.

The sale price includes $6.6 million to be split between Fenton and the U.S. government, and a 15 percent commission to be shared between Sothebys and the coin auction house, Stack's.

Fore said the auction proceeds will go into the Treasury. "It will be used to pay down the public debt and fund the war on terrorism," she said.

The coin thrills the imagination of collectors.

"It's an enigma," said Stephen Tebo, a real estate developer and coin collector from Boulder, Colorado, who dropped out of the auction when bidding topped $4 million. "It's something very, very special."

©Teacher Created Resources, Inc.

Gold Coin Sells for Millions

Use facts from the article to complete each of the following statements:

1. The 1933 Double Eagle is . . .
   a. worth $7.59.
   b. the world's most valuable coin.
   c. on sale at the U.S. Mint.
2. Thousands of Double Eagles were . . .
   a. minted in 1933.
   b. valued at $20.
   c. Both *a* and *b* are correct.
3. The rare gold coin features a picture of . . .
   a. a pair of birds.
   b. the Statue of Liberty.
   c. an eagle.
4. The Double Eagles were never circulated because President Franklin D. Roosevelt . . .
   a. took the U.S. off the gold standard.
   b. wanted the coins for his collection.
   c. thought the coins were of poor quality.
5. In 1937, all the unused Double Eagles were . . .
   a. ordered melted down.
   b. reported missing.
   c. given to the Smithsonian Institution.
6. In 1944, it was discovered that several of the coins . . .
   a. had been stolen.
   b. were being circulated in New York.
   c. could be found in Egyptian museums.
7. Nine of the missing 1933 Double Eagles were . . .
   a. owned by King Farouk.
   b. recovered.
   c. never found.
8. After disappearing for decades, one of the coins was . . .
   a. spotted at a Sotheby auction.
   b. mailed to a Secret Service agent.
   c. offered for sale by a British coin dealer.
9. The prized 1933 Double Eagle sold for . . .
   a. much more than its estimated worth.
   b. a little less than its face value.
   c. nearly as much as the Mint predicted.
10. Collectors consider the coin an "enigma" because . . .
    a. no one will ever know its true story.
    b. it has a strange appearance.
    c. an anonymous bidder now owns it.

The Price of Fame

At the time it was minted, the 1933 Double Eagle contained gold equal to its face value of $20. Assuming the coin contains an ounce of gold, what would its actual value be today? You'll find the answer in the business section of your local newspaper. Why do you think the coin sold for $7.59 million?

Thailand Bakery Adds Fish to Ice Cream

SINGBURI, Thailand (AP) — Specialty ice creams can be concocted from soy milk, olive oil and even cheese. But for the truly bizarre, come to central Thailand where a bakery is putting snakehead fish in its frozen desserts.

Kaesara Bakery's ice cream contains 40 percent fish meat, but you wouldn't know it from the smell, taste or texture. The bits of fish could easily be mistaken for coconut flakes.

The bakery, in Singburi province, where snakeheads are a culinary pride, is about to open a third outlet and expand its line of snakehead confections with fish cookies and Chinese pastries filled with deep-fried snakehead bones.

The shop's first snakehead product was a sweet-smelling cake baked in a fish-shaped mold. The key was blending four herbs for a secret syrup that eradicates the fishiness.

The cakes have been a hit since their debut at the annual Singburi Snakehead Festival seven years ago. Now the bakery, 80 miles north of Bangkok, sells some 4,000 cakes during weekends for 150 baht (US $3.50) each.

Kasara Thepprasit, the bakery's entrepeneur, said she declined an Australian company's $695,000 offer for her recipe.

"We want Thailand to have a good product that other countries don't have," Kasara said. "We didn't do this just for the money. We wanted to do this to promote Thailand and its food."

The idea to bake cakes out of fish was spawned by her husband, Supot Prasongsuksan, who wanted something special for members of Thailand's much-revered royal family when they visit the province. The bluebloods generally stop to chat with residents and are showered with gifts of the best local produce.

"Every time the royal family comes here, we give them snakehead fish cake, and they always stop to talk to me," Kasara said. "They tell me that it's good to see Thais being so inventive and creating such strange foods with just local ingredients."

Fish Is Bakery's Secret Ingredient

Use facts from the article to complete each of the following statements:

1. Kasara Thepprasit owns a . . .
   a. travel business. b. bakery in central Thailand. c. Bangkok fish market.
2. The bakery's entrepreneur (businessperson) prepares . . .
   a. cakes made with snakeheads. b. odd-tasting foods. c. cheese-flavored frozen desserts.
3. Kasara's specialty ice creams are made with . . .
   a. 40 kinds of meat. b. pieces of fish. c. soy milk and olive oil.
4. Four herbs are added to the bizarre food to . . .
   a. bring out their coconut flavor. b. add a meaty taste to the concoctions. c. get rid of the fishy smell.
5. An Australian company offered to . . .
   a. give Kasara's husband a job. b. buy the secret dessert recipe. c. pay $695,000 for 4,000 cakes.
6. Supot Prasongsuksan came up with the idea of adding fish to bakery items because he . . .
   a. knew it was a good way to earn money. b. liked to show off. c. thought it would impress the bluebloods.
7. The original snakehead product was . . .
   a. baked in a fish-shaped mold. b. intended as a gift to Thailand's royal family. c. Both *a* and *b* are correct.
8. Thais were first able to purchase cakes baked out of fish . . .
   a. at an annual Singburi Snakehead Festival. b. only on weekends. c. seventy years ago.
9. The royal family thinks that baking with snakeheads . . .
   a. keeps the tourists out of the province. b. will increase the price of cakes to $3.50 each. c. is an interesting way to use local ingredients.
10. The popular Singburi bakery plans to sell . . .
    a. cookies for fish. b. Chinese confections made with bones. c. deep-fried snake.

Grand Opening

Imagine that Kasara Thepprasit hired you to design a full-page newspaper ad for the grand opening of her third outlet. Create a colorful, easy-to-read announcement. Let readers know about the newest offerings: fish cookies and bone-filled Chinese pastries. Include an opening-day special, and be sure to list prices in baht, the currency of Thailand!

San Francisco Trolley Popular Again

SAN FRANCISCO, Calif. (AP) — They're the streetcars named desirable—again.

While tourists and residents alike "Ooh" and "Ahh" over the city's famous cable cars, the clickety-clack of a rival has proven popular on the streets of San Francisco.

Vintage trolleys—once close to extinction—are a transportation workhorse slowly making a comeback here and around the nation.

The electric trolley was introduced in the late 1800s and signaled a new mobility for working-class people formerly confined to their neighborhoods. By 1917, there were nearly 45,000 miles of track nationwide.

San Francisco's 17 cars were designed in the 1930s at the request of presidents of electric car companies in the United States and Canada who wanted standardized, improved, streamlined street cars.

That's what they got—cars that were among the sturdiest and most reliable transit vehicles ever made.

Then, with the advent of gasoline-powered buses and underground subways, most cities gradually dropped trolleys. They still operate in Boston; Newark, N.J.; Toronto; and Philadelphia.

But only in New Orleans and San Francisco are the trolleys—usually called streetcars by city natives—a major transportation force.

"There's a real tradition of rail transit here," said Dave Pharr, a trolley car fan. "Almost everybody who was born and raised here rode to school or rode to work on a street car or a cable car and maybe still does."

For San Francisco, embracing vintage trolleys has also proven to be smart public policy. The city imported nine used streetcars from Italy for about $32,000 each; a new car costs more than $2 million.

Fans hope the classic trolleys become as popular with tourists as the cable cars, the Golden Gate Bridge and the city's fog.

 ©Teacher Created Resources, Inc.

Streetcars Make a Comeback

Use facts from the article to complete each of the following statements:

1. In the late 1800s, electric trolleys . . .
   a. provided transportation for workhorses.
   b. were introduced in the United States.
   c. Both *a* and *b* are correct.
2. After cities began operating buses and subways, . . .
   a. trolley service was not needed.
   b. children had trouble getting to school.
   c. people never left their neighborhoods.
3. Vintage trolleys have become . . .
   a. extinct.
   b. the property of car company presidents.
   c. popular in a few cities around the nation.
4. Although not a major means of transportation, street cars still run in . . .
   a. New Orleans.
   b. Boston and Toronto.
   c. thousands of cities nationwide.
5. In the 1930s, San Francisco cars were . . .
   a. designed to travel on 45,000 miles of track.
   b. built to last.
   c. called streamers.
6. The California city . . .
   a. bought nine used streetcars from Italy.
   b. spent $32,000 on new tracks.
   c. charged riders $2 million.
7. In San Francisco, many people . . .
   a. ride trolleys.
   b. own cable cars.
   c. "ooh" and "ahh" over tourists.
8. Classic trolleys may have made a comeback because they . . .
   a. make clickety-clack sounds.
   b. provide riders with fans.
   c. remind people of the past.
9. Dave Pharr believes that . . .
   a. only residents should be allowed to use cable cars.
   b. everyone should ride a train to work.
   c. the cars are a part of San Francisco's history.
10. According to the story, fans hope that the old cars will . . .
    a. transport travelers over the Golden Gate Bridge.
    b. operate safely in foggy weather.
    c. become a popular tourist attraction.

Tour Guide

Imagine that you were the director of tourism in your town. Think of five attractions that would be of interest to visitors. Then design a simple brochure promoting the sites you've selected. What is your town most famous for? Are there any trolleys nearby?

U.S. Adds Color to $20 Bill

WASHINGTON, D.C. (AP) — American greenbacks have gotten a bit more colorful. A touch of peach, blue and yellow along with the traditional green and black are featured on the new $20 bill, the first to be colorized in a project to thwart counterfeiters.

The Treasury Department Bureau of Engraving and Printing, which makes the nation's paper currency, took the wrappers off the redesigned $20.

The $20 bill is the most-counterfeited note in the United States.

On both the front and back of the new $20, moving from left to right, there's a faint wash of green tint, then peach down the middle, then green again in what had been the neutral-colored background of the old notes.

The image of Andrew Jackson, the seventh president, appears slightly bigger because more of his neck and shoulders are in view and the border around his oval portrait has been removed. But his head is the same size on the new bill.

The new design also includes a faint blue eagle in the background on the front of the bill to the left of Jackson's image and a metallic green eagle and shield to the right of Jackson. Also on the front, hovering near the eagle and shield, are the words "Twenty USA" printed in a faint blue.

On the back, the White House still dominates the new $20, but a border once around the image is gone. Also, tiny number 20s are printed on the back in yellow, floating in the background.

"The White House, numbers and border have always been green and will continue to be green no matter what tint we put on there. It will always be a greenback," said Tom Ferguson, bureau director.

The new $20 also features more distinct color-shifting ink. The number "20" in the lower right corner on the front of the note changes from copper to green when the note is tilted.

Some anti-counterfeiting features included in the bill's last redesign, in 1998, are retained. They include watermarks, visible when held up to light, and embedded plastic security threads, also visible when held up to light. The words "USA Twenty" and a small flag can be seen along the thread.

The New Color of Money

Use facts from the article to complete each of the following statements:

1. U.S. paper currency is made . . .
   a. by the Bureau of Engraving and Printing.
   b. from old candy wrappers.
   c. to attract counterfeiters.
2. U.S. bank notes are known as greenbacks because of the . . .
   a. green features on the back of the bills.
   b. color-shifting ink.
   c. dollar signs around the edge of the note.
3. The new $20 bill is . . .
   a. twice the size of the old bank note.
   b. one of the easiest bills to copy.
   c. the first U.S. currency to be colorized.
4. The front of the redesigned paper money has . . .
   a. a bright blue background.
   b. images of seven presidents.
   c. pale shades of color.
5. Changes made to the back of the $20 include the . . .
   a. addition of tiny yellow number 20s.
   b. removal of the White House.
   c. appearance of floating clouds.
6. On both sides of the new currency, the background . . .
   a. is neutral-colored.
   b. has faint tints of green and peach.
   c. changes color if the bill is tilted.
7. Andrew Jackson's portrait looks slightly larger on the revised $20 because . . .
   a. the president's head has been enlarged.
   b. a border surrounds his face.
   c. his neck and shoulders appear in the image.
8. The government made the $20 note more secure by adding . . .
   a. invisible watermarks.
   b. plastic security threads.
   c. glow-in-the-dark letters.
9. Besides the 1998 anti-counterfeiting devices, the new bill features . . .
   a. a metallic green eagle.
   b. 20 copper-tinted numbers.
   c. small flags in the lower right corner.
10. One way to find out if a $20 bill is counterfeit is to . . .
    a. hold it up to the light.
    b. check for the words "USA Twenty."
    c. Both *a* and *b* are correct.

Visit the Money Factory

You can see the new $20 bill in full color on the Net at *www.moneyfactory.gov.* The home page can take you where you want to go. Choose the words "Learn all about it" for a close-up look at the new note. And, for an enhanced view of the security features, hit "interactive $20." Want to know how to detect a counterfeit bill? The answer is just a click away!

Sandwich Family Back in Business

LONDON, England (AP) — The family that invented the sandwich is back in the business. Orlando Montagu, descendant of the fourth Earl of Sandwich, opened his shop seeking a slice of London's booming luncheon trade.

The family name will be a big help: Montagu's father is the 11th Earl of Sandwich, who can trace his line directly to the man who first married beef to bread.

"There are 250 years of expectation on us," Montagu said, in his kitchen in East London. "We have tremendous pressure on us to get this right."

Earl of Sandwich, as the company is known, is starting small—a lunchtime delivery service for London's business district.

But Montagu hopes one day to open kitchens across the United Kingdom, Europe, and eventually, the world. He is backed by Robert Earl, creator of Planet Hollywood, who is the investing $2 million in the venture.

"I think it's fair to say that never in the history of brand launches has there been a brand with such awareness," said Earl.

The 18th-century John Montagu, the fourth Earl of Sandwich, is recognized as the inventor of the meal that bears his name. He is said to have wanted a quick, easy meal—so he could continue with either an all-night gambling stint or with his paperwork at a government desk, depending on the version of the story—and so put together a slice of salt beef on bread.

Orlando, his 30-year-old descendant, is trying to reclaim his family name with the launching of his company. There are Earl of Sandwich motels, restaurants, pubs and catering services scattered throughout the world but unconnected to the family.

Montagu recalled walking into a sandwich shop in Milan, Italy, in 1991 and seeing pictures of himself and his family tacked to the walls. There was even a ham and cheese sandwich named "Orlando" after him.

With more than two billion commercial sandwiches consumed each year in Britain, Montagu wanted in on the business.

"The idea has evolved over the years," said the 11th Earl of Sandwich, John Montagu, who is president of the company and a member of the House of Lords. "We always talked about sandwiches and said, 'We ought to be part of this because this is part of our family business.'"

 ©Teacher Created Resources, Inc.

Sandwich Business Is a Family Affair

Use facts from the article to complete each of the following statements:

1. The fourth Earl of Sandwich . . .
   a. trained bears in his spare time. b. owned a hotel in London. c. was named John Montagu.
2. According to the story, the 18th-century earl . . .
   a. invented the sandwich. b. was the first to salt beef. c. Both *a* and *b* are correct.
3. When the fourth earl put together the new meat-and-bread combination, he was . . .
   a. following a family recipe. b. getting ready to open a restaurant. c. looking for a quick, easy meal.
4. Orlando Montagu is . . .
   a. the father of the 11th Earl of Sandwich. b. related to the fourth earl. c. a member of the House of Lords.
5. When in a sandwich shop in Italy, Montagu discovered . . .
   a. ham and cheese was not on the menu. b. his waiter's name was Orlando. c. a sandwich was named after him.
6. The 30-year-old descendent spotted pictures of himself and his family . . .
   a. tacked to the wall of a British motel. b. on display in a Milan restaurant. c. hanging in a London pub.
7. The 11th earl's son . . .
   a. decided to start a sandwich business. b. has been working in his kitchen for 50 years. c. wants nothing to do with his family.
8. The company, known as Earl of Sandwich, . . .
   a. began operating in 1991. b. plans to make a \$2 million profit. c. offers delivery service.
9. Montagu's family name should help him to . . .
   a. attract customers from London's business district. b. make quick deliveries. c. sell 2 billion sandwiches a week.
10. It is likely that lunchtime customers expect the best because . . .
    a. Montagu's father is the company's president. b. the family invented the sandwich 250 years ago. c. Earl of Sandwich kitchens are all over the world.

Sandwich Maker

Imagine that Orlando Montagu agreed to feature your favorite sandwich on his menu. He'll want to know what it looks like and exactly how to make it. Draw a picture of the tasty hand-held meal. Include a detailed description of its ingredients. Would you want the sandwich to be named after you?

Fungus is Largest Living Thing

CORVALLIS, Oregon, (AP) — Walking through the Malheur National Forest in eastern Oregon you would be hard-pressed to notice it. But a fungus spreading through the roots of trees now covers 2,200 acres, making it the largest living organism ever found.

Popularly known as the honey mushroom, the *Armillaria ostoyae* started from a single spore too small to see without a microscope and has been weaving its black shoestring filaments through the forest for an estimated 2,400 years, killing trees as it grows.

"When you're on the ground, you don't notice the pattern; you just see dead trees in clusters," said Tina Dreisbach, a botanist and mycologist with the U.S. Forest Service's Pacific Northwest Research Station.

The outline of the giant fungus, which looks like a mushroom, stretches 3.5 miles across, and extends an average of three feet into the ground. It covers an area as big as 1,665 football fields. No one has estimated its weight.

"There hasn't been anything measured with any scientific technique that has shown any plant or animal to be larger than this," said Gregory Filip, associate professor of integrated forest protection at Oregon State University and an expert in *Armillaria.*

Until now, the largest known organism was another *Armillaria ostoyae* found in 1992 in Washington State. It covered 1,500 acres near Mount Adams.

"We just decided to go out looking for one bigger than the last," Filip said.

Forest Service scientists are interested in learning to control Armillaria because it kills trees, Filip said, but they also realize the fungus has served a purpose in nature for millions of years.

The discovery came in 1998 after Catherine Parks, a scientist at the Pacific Northwest Research Station in La Grande, Oregon, heard about a big tree that died from root rot in the forest east of Prairie City, Oregon.

Using aerial photos, Parks staked out an area of dying trees and collected root samples from 112. She identified the fungus through DNA testing. Then, by comparing cultures of the fungus grown from the 112 samples, she determined that 61 were from the same organism, meaning a single fungus had grown bigger than anything anyone had ever described.

On the surface, the only evidence of the fungus are clumps of golden mushrooms that pop up in the fall when it rains.

"They are edible, but they don't taste the best," said Dreisbach. "I would put lots of butter and garlic on them."

Giant Fungus Invades Forest

Use facts from the article to complete each of the following statements:

1. A huge fungus was discovered in Oregon . . .
   a. over 2,000 years ago. b. at the Pacific Northwest Research Station. c. in Malheur National Forest.
2. After hearing about a big tree die-off in the National Forest, scientist Catherine Parks . . .
   a. took a few courses at Oregon State University. b. collected and tested 112 root samples. c. took photographs of all the dead trees.
3. Parks discovered that 61 of the samples . . .
   a. couldn't be identified through DNA testing. b. were too small to see. c. came from the same organism.
4. The *Armillaria ostoyae*, or honey mushroom, in Oregon is . . .
   a. the largest living thing ever found. b. about the size of a football. c. very easy to notice.
5. The giant organism started . . .
   a. from a single, tiny spore (cell). b. growing 2,400 years ago. c. Both *a* and *b* are correct.
6. Armillaria extends into the ground by growing structures that look like . . .
   a. yellow leaves. b. black shoestring filaments (threads). c. bunches of rotting roots.
7. As it spreads, the giant fungus . . .
   a. reaches heights of three feet. b. weaves colorful patterns in the soil. c. kills trees.
8. The mushroom-like mass . . .
   a. covers 22,000 acres of land. b. is bigger than 1,600 football fields. c. measures 35 miles across.
9. A fungus uncovered in 1992 in Washington State was . . .
   a. bigger than Oregon's Armillaria. b. located 1,500 miles from Mount Adams. c. the largest known organism at that time.
10. Forest Service scientists hope to find a way to . . .
    a. control the spread of Armillaria. b. get rid of all types of fungi. c. keep a tree alive for a million years.

Be a Mycologist: Study Fungi

Although fungi cause plant and animal diseases, they can also be very useful. Look in an encyclopedia to find out how fungi help the soil. How are fungi useful in industry? What are some medical uses for the organisms? Have you ever eaten a fungus? Explain.

Scientist Says He Found Lost Island

SANTA BARBARA, Calif. (AP) — A scientist says he has discovered a tiny island submerged off the central California coast, more than 16,000 years after it slipped from view during the waning years of the last Ice Age.

The island, little more than a mile in length, lies 400 feet underwater about a dozen miles from shore.

It poked no more than 30 feet above the waves during the late Pleistocene, when the continental-sized ice sheets that capped much of Earth began to melt, raising global sea levels.

At that time, the four Channel Islands off Santa Barbara formed a single, larger island, called Santarosae.

Ed Keller, a University of California Santa Barbara scientist, discovered Santarosae's smaller neighbor while poring over topographic maps of the Santa Barbara Channel, a seismically active region crisscrossed with faults.

The discovery is a reminder of how advances in science—in this case, sonar technology—can restore to view land masses thought lost thousands of years ago.

"It's magnificent. We're just seeing some fantastic, very interesting things we thought we couldn't see or couldn't conceive of," said H. Gary Greene, a research scientist at the Monterey Bay Aquarium Research Institute, which mapped the region in 1998 with a shipboard sonar.

The new maps show the protrusion at near-photographic resolution.

Keller spotted the unusual uprising while examining a ridge in the middle of the channel. Unlike the comparatively smooth ocean bottom around it, the protrusion was marked by features that suggested it had been pounded by waves, rain and wind—something that could have occurred only if it had once stuck up above sea level.

"It had enough of the features that we suspected it was an island," said Keller, a professor of geological sciences and environmental studies. He dubbed his discovery "Calafia," after a mythical queen who ruled over the race of Amazons who inhabited the island of California in a popular 16th century Spanish romance novel.

Keller said Calafia was one of about 26 islands and islets thought to exist off the California coast at the peak of the last Ice Age. Today, there are about 16 separate land masses.

The island likely vanished thousands of years before the first humans arrived in Southern California. At that time, buffalo, saber-tooth cats, camels and mammoths still roamed the region.

Underwater Island Discovered

Use facts from the article to complete each of the following statements:

1. A tiny California island . . .
   a. disappeared into the Pacific Ocean.
   b. surfaced near San Miguel.
   c. was found by scientist Ed Keller.
2. A picture of the submerged island was . . .
   a. revealed on newly created topographical maps.
   b. taken at the Monterey Bay Aquarium.
   c. found floating in the Santa Barbara Channel.
3. When looking at the new maps, Keller spotted . . .
   a. an underwater structure with weather-beaten features.
   b. a 31-mile-long uprising.
   c. buffalo, saber-toothed cats and mammoths.
4. The newly discovered island . . .
   a. measures 400 feet long.
   b. is 12 miles off the coast of California.
   c. lies one mile underwater.
5. The last time "Calafia" rose above water was . . .
   a. before the late Pleistocene.
   b. more than 16,000 years ago.
   c. in 1998.
6. A long time ago, huge sheets of ice . . .
   a. covered much of Earth.
   b. formed 30 feet below the ocean floor.
   c. were located with sonar technology.
7. Melting masses of continental-sized ice caused . . .
   a. sea levels around the world to rise.
   b. submerged land forms to poke out of the ocean.
   c. many people to lose their homes.
8. At the peak of the Ice Age, the four Channel Islands off Santa Barbara . . .
   a. formed one large land mass.
   b. were known as Santarosae.
   c. Both *a* and *b* are correct.
9. There are fewer islands off the coast of California today than there were during the last ice age because . . .
   a. many of the land forms were destroyed by volcanoes.
   b. 10 of the protrusions melted.
   c. some of the islands were covered by rising sea water.
10. You can guess California researchers were . . .
    a. disappointed by the number of photographs taken.
    b. impressed with the clarity of the sonar maps.
    c. not really sure that Calafia had vanished.

Island Hopping

The Channel Islands group is made up of eight islands. How many can you find? Using an atlas, start by locating the four Channel Islands off Santa Barbara—San Miguel, Santa Rosa, Santa Cruz and Anacapa. Then keep searching the waters of Southern California for four more land masses. Make a list of your "discoveries." Did you know that the world's largest sunflower grows on Anacapa?

Fastest-Growing Tree Not Catching On

FITZGERALD, Ga. (AP) — With leaves like elephant ears and thick green stalks, young paulownia trees evoke images of the aggressive sprouts in the fairy tale "Jack and the Beanstalk."

But so far the Asian trees, described as the world's fastest-growing, have been slow to catch on in the United States.

Some tout the trees, which can grow more than 20 feet a year, as a perfect alternative for Southern farmers looking to replace tobacco. Skeptics, however, refer to them as "emus with roots," a reference to the 1990s debacle when people invested millions in large, flightless birds only to find there was no market for the meat.

"The tree grows extremely fast," said Tim Traugott, a Mississippi State University forester. "The wood doesn't shrink. You can drive nails into it and it doesn't split. It's very light wood, but relatively strong."

Paulownia trees were introduced in the United States in about 1850, possibly from seeds mixed in with packing material from Asia. They spread from New Jersey to the Carolinas as wild trees. Now there are approximately 10,000 acres grown commercially, mostly in Southeastern and Middle Atlantic states.

The trees produce light, strong wood that is used to make furniture and musical instruments such as violins and dulcimers. They can also be used to make plywood and molding.

"It's a beautiful wood," said David Drexler, who grows them on his Georgia farm. "There's really something here. It's not just a fad."

Drexler, who sells seedlings over the Internet, has several paulownia groves in his 300-acre farm. His largest trees have grown to a height of 35 to 40 feet in four years.

Former President Carter has 15 acres of paulownias near his home in Plains.

"Don't put your face over it. You may get a mouthful of leaves," he recently joked, referring to its fast growth.

But unlike pine trees, which are the mainstay of the South's timber industry, paulownias need considerable care during their first few years. Growers cut them down to the stump after the first year and they regenerate. Paulownias need dry soil and much sunshine.

 ©Teacher Created Resources, Inc.

Paulownias Set Growing Record

Use facts from the article to complete each of the following statements:

1. Paulownia is the . . .
   a. the world's fastest-growing tree.
   b. author of "Jack and the Beanstalk."
   c. Asian word for a young elephant.
2. Paulownia trees were first found growing in the United States . . .
   a. soon after New Jersey farmers ordered seeds from Asia.
   b. in the mid-19th century.
   c. on 10,000 acres of land in the Carolinas.
3. The Asian trees . . .
   a. can grow 20 feet a year.
   b. have thick, green stems.
   c. Both *a* and *b* are correct.
4. The leaves of the distinctive tree . . .
   a. look like elephant ears.
   b. have replaced tobacco.
   c. taste like meat.
5. Wood produced by the quick-sprouting tree is . . .
   a. known to have a problem with mold.
   b. most beautiful if grown in the wild.
   c. used to make furniture and musical instruments.
6. You can guess that forester Tim Traugott thinks timber from Paulownia trees . . .
   a. should be made to split easily.
   b. can be used to build many things.
   c. would grow more slowly if it were heavier.
7. The trees are . . .
   a. not very popular in the United States.
   b. home to emus, large flightless birds.
   c. often mentioned in fairy tales.
8. According to the article, tree farmer David Drexler . . .
   a. sells year-old plants over the Internet.
   b. has grown 35 feet in the last four years.
   c. owns a few Paulownia groves.
9. Former President Jimmy Carter . . .
   a. thinks the stories about Paulownia are a joke.
   b. grows the tall plants on land near his home.
   c. warns people not to eat the leaves of the tree.
10. The last paragraph of the story suggests that Paulownias . . .
    a. are a lot easier to care for than pines.
    b. will grow better if cut down after the first year.
    c. do not need water to survive.

Woodworking Project

There are many different kinds of wood. You can probably find examples of some varieties in your home. Look for things made out of birch, cherry, maple, oak, pine, teak, or walnut. Make a chart showing the results of your "scavenger" hunt. Is a dulcimer on your list? How about a toothpick?

Scientists Find Virtuosos Get an Early Start

WASHINGTON, D.C. (AP) — To become a violin virtuoso you have to start practicing by the age of 12. Thirteen is too late, say scientists who have studied the brains of musicians.

Edward Taub of the University of Alabama, Birmingham, said magnetic images of the brains of people who play stringed instruments show that larger and more complex neuron circuits form in violinists who started their training at an early age than among those who began later in life.

"There is an abrupt change between ages 12 and 13 that appears to be quite dramatic," said Taub.

Violinists who started studies between ages 3 and 12 showed no significant differences in the brain circuitry. But there was a distinctly reduced level of development, said Taub, in the brains of those who didn't start musical studies until after the age of 13.

In the study, researchers concentrated on a part of the brain cortex that detects sensory signals. Taub said specific and known parts of this brain structure receive signals from the fingers, the face and the torso. Sensations from the left side are detected on the right side of the brain and those from the right are reflected in the left side. This enables a direct comparison.

To test differences that could develop between the left and right hands, the scientists used nine musicians who play stringed instruments, such as the violin, which demand a high level of dexterity for the left hand but less for the right.

The individual fingers were then stimulated with slight pressure from an air-driven device once a second for 1,000 seconds. As this occurred, the response of the cerebral cortex was recorded and analyzed by a computer.

Similar readings were taken on six non-musicians as controls.

The most widespread and complex response in the cortex was found for the left fingers among five string players who started their training before the age of 12. For four who started training between the ages of 13 and 20, the brain activity in response to the left finger stimulation was as much as 60 percent less.

For the non-musical controls, the response was up to 80 percent less.

String players were used in the study because there is an uneven demand for dexterity between the left and right hands. When playing the violin, the fingers of the left hand move rapidly to press down strings of the instrument and thus create different notes. The main job of the right hand is to stroke with the bow, a task requiring much less finger dexterity.

Even the thumb of the left hand, whose job is mostly to hold the instrument, showed less brain development than the left fingers.

 ©Teacher Created Resources, Inc.

Brain Power

Use facts from the article to complete each of the following statements:

1. A University of Alabama study showed that most skilled musicians . . .
   a. practice three times a day. b. begin training at an early age. c. go to concerts every weekend.
2. In the study, researchers measured the brain activity of . . .
   a. people who have never played an instrument. b. people who played stringed instruments. c. Both *a* and *b* are correct.
3. The left side of the brain receives a signal from the . . .
   a. left side of the torso. b. left hand. c. right hand.
4. The scientists used a computer to . . .
   a. record and study brain information. b. measure the thumb size of musicians. c. test for intelligence.
5. Researchers discovered that fewer changes occurred in the brain circuitry of musicians who began their studies . . .
   a. before the age of 3. b. between the ages of 6 and 12. c. in their late teens.
6. Young children who are taught to play stringed instruments . . .
   a. may develop more complex brain circuitry. b. find that music lessons are easy. c. will always grow up to be musicians.
7. The brains of violin virtuosos (artists with outstanding skills) were found to be . . .
   a. a lot like computers. b. affected by magnets. c. different from those of non-musicians.
8. String players use fingering skills in order to . . .
   a. become left-handed. b. quickly press down the string of their instrument. c. get used to holding a violin.
9. Learning finger skills at an early age causes the brain to . . .
   a. become smaller in size. b. signal young children to act like teen-agers. c. form large neuron circuits.
10. By pressing down the strings on a violin, a musician can . . .
    a. make sure he doesn't drop the instrument. b. play different notes. c. keep the brain active.

What's Playing?

The four sections of an orchestra are string, woodwind, brass, and percussion. Using an encyclopedia to help you, make a list of the instruments in each section. Why not attend a concert? Check your local newspaper for listings of upcoming events.

Fossil of Monster Crocodile Found

WASHINGTON, D.C. (AP) — A crocodile longer than a school bus and weighing about 10 tons was the top predator in an African river 110 million years ago, routinely dining on large dinosaurs that came within range of its toothy jaws.

"When this thing grew into an adult it was really a monster," Paul C. Sereno, a well-known dinosaur hunter at the University of Chicago, said in an interview. "This thing could have easily pulled down a good-sized dinosaur."

Fossils of the monster croc were uncovered in a desert in Niger by Sereno and his team. The species, called *Sarcosuchus imperator,* or "flesh crocodile emperor," was first discovered by French scientists in 1964, but the Sereno find is the most complete fossil skeleton known.

"This new material gives us a good look at hyper-giant crocodiles," said Sereno in a statement. "No one had enough of the skull and skeleton to really nail any of the true croc giants until now."

Sereno said that the elongated skull of the Sarcosuchos (pronounced SARK-oh-SOOK-us) is about six feet in length and dominated by narrow jaws studded with more than 100 teeth. The upper jaw, tipped with large, sharp and powerful incisors, overlaps the lower jaw, an ideal design to lock and hold onto flesh.

"The teeth are incredibly stout," he said. "They are crushing, penetrating teeth," which means the animal probably fed on land animals more than on fish and turtles, the most common food of modern crocodiles and alligators.

Sereno said the animal's eye sockets are rotated upward, enabling it to remain submerged in water while watching the shoreline.

"This suggests it was an ambush predator, hiding under the water and then surging out to grab anything lounging on the shore," he said.

Modern crocodiles living in African rivers often grab large animals, such as wildebeest and zebras, and drag them into the water where they are drowned and then torn apart.

Sarcosuchus probably did the same thing, said Sereno, but because the ancient animal was so large it could easily handle huge dinosaurs, including the massive long-necked, small-headed sauropods that were common in that African region.

"A small sauropod, 20 or 30 feet in length, would have been no problem," said Sereno. He said the giant crock probably remained still in the water until an animal came to drink and then it whipped its jaws out and sunk its teeth into its prey.

"And that would have been it," Sereno said. "Once one of these clamped onto the leg or neck of an animal, there wasn't a lot it [the victim] could do."

 ©Teacher Created Resources, Inc.

Giant Crocodile Dined on Dinosaurs

Use facts from the article to complete each of the following statements:

1. Fossils of a huge crocodile were found . . .
   a. on the shore of a river in Niger.
   b. in an African desert.
   c. 110 million years ago.
2. Dinosaur hunter Paul C. Sereno . . .
   a. discovered the giant crocodile skeleton.
   b. wasn't able to find the monster's head.
   c. said that the creature's bones weighed 10 tons.
3. The skull of the Sarcosuchus . . .
   a. is 6 feet wide.
   b. weighs as much as a school bus.
   c. has a long, narrow shape.
4. The upper jaw of the hyper-giant reptile . . .
   a. contains more than 1,000 teeth.
   b. sticks out over the lower jaw.
   c. Both *a* and *b* are correct.
5. According to the story, the ancient "emperor" was able to . . .
   a. roll its eyes around to the back of its head.
   b. stay underwater for a long time.
   c. take its teeth out of its mouth.
6. Sereno believes the river-dwelling croc probably ate land animals because it . . .
   a. didn't know how to catch fish.
   b. had very strong teeth.
   c. made its home near a river.
7. The flesh-eating crocodile is described as an ambush predator because it . . .
   a. hid in the water and waited to attack.
   b. was covered with greenish-brown scales.
   c. only ate live animals.
8. The adult croc most likely captured a sauropod by . . .
   a. waiting for the dinosaur to take a swim.
   b. breaking the neck of its prey.
   c. locking its incisors onto the animal's flesh.
9. Modern crocodiles are similar to Sarcosuchus because they . . .
   a. eat good-sized dinosaurs.
   b. capture wildebeest and zebras.
   c. drown their prey.
10. You can guess that Sereno's discovery is important because . . .
   a. the fossils show that the ancient beast was huge.
   b. now scientists can finally stop searching for bones.
   c. no one had ever heard of the species before.

Croc Snapshot

Imagine a giant crocodile surging out of the water to grab a massive long-necked, small-headed sauropod. Draw an action-packed picture of what you "see." Use the descriptive words in the story to help you create a "snapshot" from the past of a Sarcosuchus in its habitat. Remember to include a lot of teeth!

Slurping Food a No-No in Japan

TOKYO, Japan (AP) — Akimasa Matsushima is a well-educated man. He considers himself polite. And when he eats his noodles, at home or in a restaurant, he does it with a hearty "SHLLURRPP."

Slurping loud and long is what Matsushima and most Japanese over 40 were taught was the polite way to eat hot noodles and just about anything else slurp-able.

Now, it's almost a declaration of war.

"It used to be normal to make noises while eating," Matsushima, a 56-year-old lawyer, said self-consciously over dinner recently at a Tokyo noodle shop where he and a few other slurpers broke the quiet ambiance.

The battle is between generations, and genders.

Many middle-aged and older Japanese believe noodles taste better if slurped quickly while they're hot and drenched in broth. A loud slurp is also a way of showing you are enjoying the meal.

But younger Japanese are more concerned not to dribble the soup onto their silk ties and Gucci dresses. Reared on Western manners and a more Western diet, they are likely to be offended when those around them slurp.

"Slurping is for old men," said Riki Kishida, a 32-year-old accountant eating at the same restaurant as Matsushima. "Slurping has nothing to do with whether it tastes good or not."

Japan's ubiquitous noodle restaurants have yet to set up no-slurping sections. But the simmering skirmish has not been lost on Japanese social commentators and editorial writers.

Clearly siding with the older generation, an editorial on the front page of the *Asahi*, a major newspaper, lamented the silence of the noodles.

"It'll be a truly lonely feeling when nobody makes any slurping noises at all," it said.

Many factors have been cited.

One is that Japanese eating habits have changed, said Tamami Kondo, principal of the privately-owned Seishikai Etiquette Academy in Tokyo.

Kondo said children, under the watch of younger, non-slurping mothers or teachers, are as likely to eat pasta or a burger as noodles. When they do eat noodles, she said, they may well wrap them around their chopsticks spaghetti-style.

Either way, they learn from an early age that slurping is a no-no.

 ©Teacher Created Resources, Inc.

Noisy Noodles

Use facts from the article to complete each of the following statements:

1. Many older Japanese slurp . . .
   a. while eating or drinking. b. when buying hot sauce. c. to show they are well-educated.
2. To slurp means to . . .
   a. make loud, sucking sounds. b. yell across the table. c. talk too much.
3. In Japan, most people over 40 were taught . . .
   a. never to buy noodles in a restaurant. b. that it's polite to make noises while eating. c. not to swallow hot soup.
4. Akimasa Matsushima thinks that when he slurps he . . .
   a. shows he is enjoying his meal. b. makes the noodles taste better. c. Both *a* and *b* are correct.
5. The under-40 crowd believes making long, loud noises . . .
   a. may cause food fights. b. should be allowed in Tokyo restaurants. c. is rude.
6. Riki Kishida says . . .
   a. he dislikes noodles drenched (soaked) in broth. b. old men should eat at home. c. slurping doesn't improve the flavor of food.
7. It is likely that in some restaurants, noisy eaters . . .
   a. are seated in the no-slurping section. b. annoy the younger patrons. c. demand to be served hamburgers.
8. The older generation is probably unhappy about "the silence of the noodles" because they . . .
   a. are so used to hearing hearty slurps. b. think quiet eaters are lonely. c. enjoy dinner conversation.
9. According to the story, Japanese children learn slurping is a no-no by . . .
   a. attending Seishikai Etiquette Academy. b. watching their mothers or teachers c. eating more pasta than noodles.
10. After reading this story, you can guess that . . .
    a. the Japanese are always fighting with each other. b. spaghetti is the most popular dish in Tokyo. c. Western food has changed Japan's eating habits.

Dignified Dining

Good table manners make meals more enjoyable. Tell why each of the five rules of etiquette listed below is important. Then think of five more proper behaviors to add to the list. Have you ever slurped? Explain

- ask politely
- eat slowly
- say thank you
- use utensils quietly
- wait patiently

True or False

General Directions

Use information from the Associated Press articles to answer "True" or "False" to the statements. Write "True" or "False" on the lines next to each statement or record your answers on the "True and False Worksheet" (page 107).

Suggested Directions to the Student:

1. Read the headline to get a clue about the topic of the story.
2. Number the paragraphs. Whenever possible, find paragraph proof for your answers.
3. Read the *entire* story before answering the questions.
4. Use the context of the story to figure out the meaning of unfamiliar words.
5. Use facts from the story to determine if a statement is true or false. No additional information is needed to answer the questions.
6. Although facts are presented out of sequence, answer questions in order, rereading parts of the story to verify information. (Ask, "Where in the article was the author looking when she wrote this statement?")
7. The true or false skill is similar to the multiple choice exercise in that a statement is true only if *all* of the information contained in the sentence is correct according to the article.
8. True statements restate information found in the article, using different words to express the same ideas that were presented by the author.
9. If a statement is correct, just write "True" in the answer space on your worksheet.
10. If the statement is incorrect, write "False," and then rewrite the sentence to make it true using as many of the original words as possible.
11. For rewritten statements, underline the part of the sentence that was changed or added to in order to make the statement true.
12. The bonus question is an inferential statement based on facts from the story. The ideas in the sentence are not directly stated in the article.
13. Use the supplemental activity to expand upon ideas presented in the story.

Teachers Note: If you prefer, you may choose to have students write "T" for "True" and "F" for "False" on their worksheet....

True or False Worksheet

Student Name: ______________________________ **Date:** ________

Column Title: ______________________________

	Paragraph Proof	True or False	Rewritten Statement
1.			
2.			
3.			
4.			
5.			
6.			
7.			
8.			
9.			
10.			

Score Box [ ]

Tyke with Toy Strikes Dino Pay Dirt

ALBUQUERQUE, N.M. (AP) — Don Shiffler didn't think much about it when his 3-year-old son insisted that the thin, green rock he unearthed with his toy backhoe was a dinosaur egg.

Think again, Dad. Researchers say the "rock" young David Shiffler found is the oldest evidence of a meat-eating egg-laying dinosaur.

The family was on their way home from a camping trip, having just seen *The Land Before Time*, a cartoon about a little dinosaur, and Shiffler said David had dinosaurs on the mind.

"Everything he picked up that day was a dinosaur egg," said Shiffler. He put the fragment on a shelf in the family garage for nearly two months.

David kept telling his father that the coin-sized fragment, which he dug up near Rio Puerco, west of Albuquerque, was important.

"I knew it was a dinosaur egg," David, now 4, said during a news conference at the New Mexico Museum of Natural History and Science, where the fossilized piece of eggshell is now displayed.

After Dad gave in and took the piece to the museum, researchers there sent it to Emily Bray, a University of Colorado paleontologist. She determined that it was a one-of-a-kind find, which is changing scientists' theories of when meat-eating egg-laying dinosaurs first appeared.

The fragment, about 150 million years old, gives more evidence that meat-eating—or therapod—dinosaurs laid hard-shelled eggs during the upper Jurassic period, Bray said.

It also could prove that dinosaur eggs from that era were hard-shelled, not leathery, advancing the theory that modern birds are descendants of dinosaurs.

Spencer Lucas, a paleontologist at the New Mexico museum, said the oldest meat-eating dinosaur egg previously found in North America came from the Cretaceous period, about 70 million years ago.

Fossilized eggshells are rare in the Southwest because the region was very wet during the time of the dinosaurs, and eggs usually don't fossilize in such an environment.

 ©Teacher Created Resources, Inc.

Boy Discovers Dinosaur Egg

Use information from the story to answer **True** or **False** to the following statements. Write **T** or **F** on the line next to each statement.

__________ 1. David Shiffler found an old toy when digging with his backhoe near the family garage.

__________ 2. David made his discovery when he was three years old.

__________ 3. After watching a cartoon about a dinosaur, the boy imagined that many of the rocks he found were dinosaur eggs.

__________ 4. As soon as the boy's father, Don Shiffler, took a look at the green rock, he knew it was a fossil.

__________ 5. It took almost two months for the tot to convince his dad to take the fragment (piece) to the New Mexico museum.

__________ 6. Researchers at the New Mexico Museum of Natural History and Science believe that the eggshell is worth a quarter.

__________ 7. Paleontologist Emily Bray, who studies prehistoric life, figured that the piece was 150 million years old.

__________ 8. David's "rock" is proof that all dinosaurs laid hard-shelled eggs.

__________ 9. Some scientists think that modern birds may have originally come from dinosaurs.

__________ 10. The fossilized eggshell can be seen at the University of Colorado.

__________ **Bonus:** The first dinosaur egg unearthed in North America was found nearly 70 million years ago.

Dinosaur Dilemma

At first, Don Shiffler didn't think much about his son's discovery. Using facts from the story, make a list of four possible reasons why David's dad didn't take him seriously. Would you have thought the green rock was important? Why do you think David's father finally gave in?

Lost Wallet Turns Up After 50 Years

PETALUMA, Calif. (AP) — A San Francisco police officer who works at the same station his grandfather once did more than 50 years ago received an unusual package in the mail.

It was his grandfather's wallet—complete with identification, business cards and $60.

In 1951, John Payne, a retired San Francisco police officer, was buying produce in Bakersfield when he left his wallet in a phone booth.

He died four years later without telling his family about the lost wallet. It arrived at the police station along with a letter from Robert Kupbens, a 79-year-old Tucson man.

The letter read: "Dear Sir, I found this wallet in a telephone booth in Bakersfield, California, in 1951. Much later I found the wallet in my personal gear and intended to send it to its owner but put it away and forgot about it in the following years because it was misplaced. Sorry it took so long to get this wallet to lost and found."

It goes on to explain how, after discovering the wallet in the phone booth, Kupbens tried to give it to a gas station attendant, but the man told him to take it to the police.

"I had to continue on my way north so I put it in a zipper bag and continued," he wrote.

But he got in an auto accident and forgot about the wallet.

The letter ends: "P.S. There were $60 in bills in the wallet. Please find a check enclosed."

John Payne II, who lives in Petaluma, called Kupbens to get the full story.

"Can you believe someone is that honest?" Payne told the *Santa Rosa Press Democrat*. "It was an emotional thing. I couldn't believe it. He had an ID card from 1942 with his picture on it."

Payne's grandfather gave up police work to enter the produce business and frequently made buying trips up and down the West Coast.

Receipts inside the black leather wallet showed he had been to the Oregon border to buy potatoes and to El Centro to buy melons.

He kept a log of trip expenses: "gas $3, eats 90 cents, room $4."

Payne barely remembers his grandfather and was thrilled to receive the wallet and learn more about him.

"The guys [at the station] cracked up because they saw the similarities. The wide forehead," he said. "We're from the same gene pool."

 ©Teacher Created Resources, Inc.

Forgotten Wallet Finally Returned

Use information from the story to answer **True** or **False** to the following statements. Write **T** or **F** on the line next to each statement.

__________ 1. More than 50 years ago, John Payne left his wallet in a phone booth in California.

__________ 2. The retired police officer was in Bakersfield because he was interested in buying a produce business.

__________ 3. A gas station attendant found the lost item.

__________ 4. Robert Kupbens wasn't able to take the black leather wallet to the police, so he tucked it away in a zipper bag.

__________ 5. When Kupbens found the wallet, it contained a photo ID, a list of travel expenses, and a check for $60.

__________ 6. According to the log, Payne didn't have enough money to buy food while on his buying trip to Oregon.

__________ 7. After getting into a car accident, Kupbens forgot all about Payne's wallet.

__________ 8. Shortly before he died, the fruit-and-vegetable dealer told his family about his lost possession.

__________ 9. The Tucson man, now 51 years old, discovered the forgotten wallet in his pants.

__________ 10. When Kupbens sent the wallet to a San Francisco police station, he had no idea Payne's grandson would get the package.

__________ **Bonus:** John Payne II was grateful that the wallet was returned because it held clues to his grandfather's past.

Price Adjustment

Traveling expenses have certainly increased over the past 50 years! Assuming prices are at least 10 times higher than they were in 1951, how much money would John Payne have listed in his log for gas, food, and hotel if he took his trip today? About how far could you travel today on $3 worth of gas?

"Bird Brain" Might Be a Compliment

CHICAGO, Ill. (AP) — Polly want an education?

Maybe Polly doesn't need one. New research seems to indicate that parrots, like chimps and dolphins, are capable of mastering complex intellectual concepts that children cannot handle until the age of 5.

Pet experts gathering in Chicago for the American Veterinary Association's annual animal welfare forum believe the parrot's intelligence is why the popularity of the bird had grown faster than that any other pet over the last decade.

Irene Pepperberg is an ecologist and evolutionary biologist who studies the intelligence of parrots. Pepperberg, of the University of Arizona in Tucson, has focused her studies on a parrot she bought at a Chicago pet store in 1977.

That bird, Alex, can name 50 objects when shown them, knows colors, knows numbers up to eight and even understands the concepts of *same* and *different*.

"All of the tests we've done with dolphins and great apes to investigate their intelligence, we've done with Alex," Pepperberg said. "He scored as well as they did in many of them, better in some."

Bird brains are different than those of advanced mammals, catching the interest of neurologists, psychologists and others.

Intelligence doesn't always equal a good pet, however.

Experts say the bird is domineering and sometimes difficult to understand, and although they can live up to 80 years, many people give up these pets after the first five years.

"I have seen entire families, their German shepherd included, buffaloed by a bird." said Chris Davis, a California parrot psychology expert. "They are never subservient."

But Liz Wilson, a parrot behavior consultant from Philadelphia, said she's heard of cases where people come home feeling blue and their parrot asks them outright, "Is something wrong?"

"You have to earn their love. I like that," she said.

Parrots Make Good Pupils

Use information from the story to answer **True** or **False** to the following statements. Write **T** or **F** on the line next to each statement.

__________ 1. Recent studies have found that parrots can understand complex (complicated) ideas.

__________ 2. Animal researchers have proven that parrots and dolphins know more than a five-year-old child.

__________ 3. Many people keep parrots as pets because the birds grow faster than most other animals.

__________ 4. Scientist Irene Pepperberg spent a number of years studying the intelligence of her parrot, Alex.

__________ 5. Pepperberg taught her bird to say the names of objects and to recognize colors.

__________ 6. The brainy bird has learned to act just like a great ape.

__________ 7. Pepperberg's educated pet scored as well as or better than chimps on some intelligence tests.

__________ 8. People who care for parrots live to be 80 years old.

__________ 9. Bird owners report that, after five years of training, the animal becomes subservient (easy to control).

__________ 10. According to the article, some pet parrots are so smart that they can tell when family members are feeling sad.

__________ **Bonus:** In order to earn a parrot's love, it is necessary to teach the bird how to speak and count.

Brainstorm

Alex can identify 50 different small objects, such as a key, ball, or pen. If you were able to work with the parrot, what items would you want the bird to recognize? How would you get it to say the name of each thing? How long do you think it would take?

More Sunken Treasure Found in Florida

KEY WEST, Fla. (AP) — The treasure hunters who discovered the gold-laden Spanish galleon *Nuestra Senora de Atocha* have found another part of the wreck that is yielding gold bars, money chains, silver coins and jewelry.

The sparkling booty, estimated to be worth $500,000, was exhibited and unloaded from a salvage vessel. The salvagers believe there could be millions of dollars more in treasure yet to be discovered.

"We think this is probably going to be bigger than the initial mother lode," said Morgan Perkins, a representative of the Fisher family.

Treasure hunter Mel Fisher, who died in 1998, found the first silver coin from the *Nuestra* in 1971. The family found the main pile in 1985.

The *Nuestra Senora*, carrying millions in gold and silver bullion, was bound for Spain from the New World when it went down in a hurricane about 30 miles west of Key West in 1622. Fisher's company, Treasure Solvers Inc., had recovered artifacts estimated to be worth $200 million to $500 million.

Mel Fisher's son, Kim Fisher, said his dive teams located the sterncastle—the galleon's rear structure, where aristocracy, the clergy and their belongings traveled—about 12 miles from the original find 15 years ago.

The latest find was made in 2000. Fisher said his crews uncovered three solid gold bars, 120 silver coins, several gold chains, a gold medallion of possible Aztec origin and assorted other pieces of Indian jewelry thought to have come from South America.

"In addition to the gold and silver, we're finding swords, cannon balls, rifles and other armaments," Fisher said.

There may be "one-of-a-kind" items still undiscovered, Perkins said. "You'll find gold chains that no one else has seen. A shipwreck is like a window into the past because it's perfectly preserved and not many of those artifacts exist today."

 ©Teacher Created Resources, Inc.

Treasure Hunters Strike It Rich

Use information from the story to answer **True** or **False** to the following statements. Write **T** or **F** on the line next to each statement.

_________ 1. In 1622, a treasure-filled Spanish galleon (sailing ship) sank off the coast of Florida.

_________ 2. The *Nuestra Senora de Atocha* was carrying millions of dollars worth of bullion (bars of gold or silver).

_________ 3. After sailing for 30 days, the Spanish ship was destroyed in a hurricane.

_________ 4. Treasure hunter Mel Fisher found the first silver coin from the downed vessel in 1985.

_________ 5. Fourteen years after locating the *Nuestra*, Fisher's company recovered treasure worth almost $200.

_________ 6. In July, another part of the wreck was discovered 12 miles from the site of the original pile of booty.

_________ 7. Divers built a sandcastle in the rear of the ship.

_________ 8. Kim Fisher's crew uncovered three gold bars and 120 silver coins.

_________ 9. Besides the sparkling treasure, swords and rifles were found onboard the boat.

_________ 10. Shipwrecks are valuable because they provide a way for researchers to learn about the past.

_________ **Bonus:** It is likely that Mel Fisher's son will continue to search the deep for "one-of-a-kind artifacts."

What's It Worth?

The price of an ounce of gold or silver is constantly changing. Look in the business section of your local newspaper to find the latest quotes on the two metals. Use the most recent values to calculate the worth of the items listed below. (Hint: 1 pound equals 16 ounces.) Would you like to be a treasure hunter?

- 3-ounce silver coin
- 1/2-ounce silver coin
- 11-ounce gold bar
- 2-pound gold bar
- 6-ounce gold chain

Satellites Measuring Washington Monument

WASHINGTON, D.C. (AP) — The Washington Monument is a bit taller than previously thought.

A team of government geodesists used satellites to take the monument's most accurate measurement ever. Their preliminary result was 555 feet, 5.9 inches. Geodesy is the science of measuring the Earth.

Previously, the height of the monument has been reported as 555 feet, 5.5 inches. It was last measured 65 years ago by government surveyors.

Scaffolding erected for a renovation of the monument gave the team from the National Oceanic and Atmospheric Administration (NOAA) access to the top of the giant stone pillar.

The team from NOAA's National Geodetic Survey took several measurements during their visit to the apex and reported final, detailed figures, NOAA officials said.

"Engineers will also use this information to monitor the monument's stability, measuring any shifting, settling, or other movement of the structure," NOAA Administrator D. James Baker said in a statement. He added that the same methods used in the project can be used for navigation and transportation and communications systems.

The geodesits used state-of-the-art Global Positioning System receivers and other specialized gear to take hundreds of measurements at the top of the monument and at several other nearby Washington landmarks.

The last official geodetic measurements from the top of the Washington Monument were made in 1934 by the U.S. Coast and Geodetic Survey, the National Geodetic Survey's predecessor agency. At that time, manual observations were made with instruments such as theodolites, spirit levels and leveling rods.

Such precise measurements are part of the Geodetic's Survey's National Spatial Reference System, which is the foundation of all types of surveys and allows government, industry and researchers to measure the position of objects in three-dimensional space.

 ©Teacher Created Resources, Inc.

Washington Monument Surveyed

Use information from the story to answer **True** or **False** to the following statements. Write **T** or **F** on the line next to each statement.

__________ 1. Geodesy is the science of measuring the Earth.

__________ 2. With the help of satellites, a team of government geodesists measured the height of the Washington Monument.

__________ 3. Scientists from the National Oceanic and Atmospheric Administration (NOAA) decided to rebuild the famous landmark.

__________ 4. Using scaffolding put up for repair of the monument, the NOAA team was able to reach the apex (top) of the structure.

__________ 5. Geodesists found that the historic column is 4 inches taller than previously thought.

__________ 6. Sixty-five years ago, government surveyors reported that the height of the stone pillar was almost 5,556 feet.

__________ 7. In 1934, measurements from the top of the Washington Monument were made with theodolites and leveling rods.

__________ 8. NOAA's National Geodetic Survey team measured the white marble obelisk hundreds of times.

__________ 9. State-of-the-art gear enabled scientists to paint perfect pictures of the Washington landmark.

__________ 10. By moving the monument, engineers can tell if the memorial is stable (secure).

__________ **Bonus:** It is possible for scientists to use satellites to accurately measure the position of objects on Earth.

Honoring Our Presidents

The Washington Monument was built in our nation's capital to honor the memory of George Washington. Visit your local library to find out which of the U.S. presidents listed below also has been honored with a memorial. Which landmark is pictured on the back of a $5 bill?

- Ulysses Grant
- Abraham Lincoln
- Thomas Jefferson
- James Madison
- Theodore Roosevelt
- John F. Kennedy

Worms in Gulf of Mexico Live Long

STATE COLLEGE, Pa. (AP) — Giant worms living 1,700 feet below the surface of the Gulf of Mexico have been found to be up to 250 years old—a record for creatures without a backbone, scientists say.

Researchers from Penn State University reported their findings in the journal *Nature*.

The tube worms, whose scientific name is *Lamellibrachia*, do not eat; they survive by absorbing energy from chemicals that seep up through cracks in the sea floor.

They grow to lengths of 10 feet or more. That's not a record for worms. That distinction goes to a tapeworm that lives in the intestines of whales.

This species is a fairly new discovery. Scientists learned about it in the 1980s. The worms live in clusters of millions, covering acres of ocean floor. Each worm is protected by a thin, flexible, shell-like tube.

Some tortoises live even longer. And marine biologist Charles Fisher said colonies of coral live for centuries. But *Lamellibrachia* holds the age record for a single invertebrate organism, he said.

Finding out the age of a giant sea worm is a bit more complex than counting the rings of a tree. Fisher and his colleagues rode a submarine to the bottom of the gulf, where they used robotic arms to mark the ends of the tubes. Three months later, they returned and measured how much the worms had grown. They kept returning and measuring every few months for four years.

Once they had that data, they were able to calculate how long it would have taken for the worms to grow to their existing lengths.

What's the secret to this longevity?

One hypotheses is that the *Lamellibrachia* worms live in an environment where they are less likely to get bruised, broken or run out of the energy they absorb.

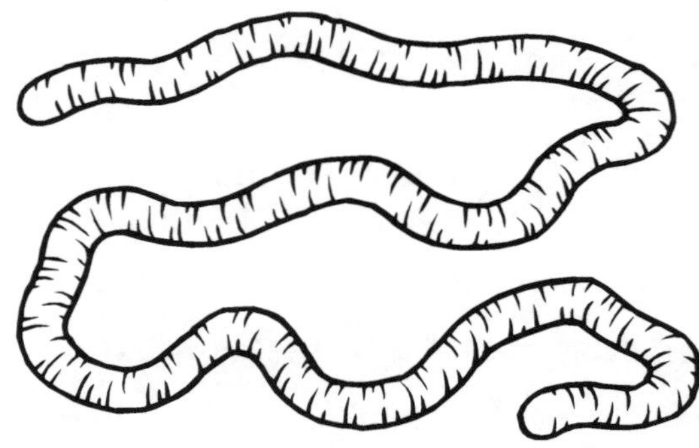

Worms Hold Age Record

Use information from the story to answer **True** or **False** to the following statements. Write **T** or **F** on the line next to each statement.

__________ 1. In the 1980s, researchers discovered 250-year-old worms living in the Gulf of Mexico.

__________ 2. Worms protected by shell-like tubes were clustered together on millions of acres of ocean floor.

__________ 3. According to the story, tube worms, or Lamellibrachia, often fall through cracks in the bottom of the gulf.

__________ 4. This newly discovered species is believed to live longer than any other invertebrate (an animal without a backbone).

__________ 5. Marine biologist Charles Fisher said he figured out the age of Lamellibrachia worms by first counting their rings.

__________ 6. Researchers from Penn State University used a robotic device to measure the length of the worms.

__________ 7. Some of the undersea creatures are 1,700 feet long.

__________ 8. The giant worms survive by absorbing (taking in) energy from chemicals in the sea.

__________ 9. Fisher found tube worms living inside whales.

__________ 10. Scientists think that one reason for the longevity of the worms might be that they live in a protected environment.

__________ **Bonus:** You can guess that finding out the age of tube worms was a difficult and challenging underwater task.

Long Live the Turtle

Turtles live longer than most other back-boned animals. Look in an encyclopedia to find out more about this reptile with a shell. When did the first turtles appear on Earth? Which turtle is the biggest? Which is the smallest? Where do turtles live? Did you know that turtles are toothless?

Researchers Say Full Moon Heats Earth a Bit

WASHINGTON, D.C. (AP) — It won't melt the snows of winter or start a moon-tanning fad; but when the moon turns its fully lighted face toward Earth, it heats the planet ever so slightly.

A study published in the journal *Science* reported that two Arizona State University researchers have used precise global temperature measurements from satellites to show that every time the moon is full, the Earth's temperature rises by .03 degrees Fahrenheit.

"Moonburn is not a problem," quipped Robert C. Balling, climate specialist at Arizona State.

While the very slight temperature rise is not enough to notice, Balling said the study does prove that moonbeams give Earth both light and warmth.

"Moonlight is very much less than the energy coming in from the sun, but there is a little bit of warming."

At its brightest, Balling said, moonshine delivers to Earth about .0102 watt of heat energy per square meter. Earth gets about 1,367 watts per square meter of constant energy from the sun, he said. A watt of energy is equal to 1/746th of one horsepower.

The moon is not creating the light and heat, but is reflecting energy from the sun and sending it 220,000 miles across space to add a romantic glow to Earth's night.

Every 29.53 days, as it orbits Earth, the moon goes through lighting phases, changing from nearly invisible to shining in all its glory.

From Earth, the full moon seems a gentle, silvery place. But up there, among the lunar craters, the moon at high noon is like an oven. The lunar surface typically sears at 200 degrees in the full sun, and Balling said that throws off enough heat to travel to Earth and warm the planet very slightly.

During the new lunar phase, the moon's sunlit side is away from the Earth. The side of the moon seen from Earth is in shadow and there is little or no energy reflected from the moon toward Earth. It was this energy difference, between the new and the full moon, that was measured.

Balling said weather and climate satellites aimed at Earth can so accurately gauge surface temperatures that it is now possible to measure the lunar heat effects.

The researchers compiled a data set of global temperatures from 1979 to 1994 and then used computers to plot the satellite readings against the lunar cycle. Balling said the results showed a consistent warming—by a fraction of a degree—during each of the full moon cycles. But, he said, the temperature rise is too insignificant to affect Earth's weather.

 ©Teacher Created Resources, Inc.

Moonlighting

Use information from the story to answer **True** or **False** to the following statements. Write **T** or **F** on the line next to each statement.

_________ 1. Arizona State researchers discovered that the full moon can warm Earth about three degrees.

_________ 2. The results of the moonlighting study were published in a scientific journal.

_________ 3. Researchers used satellite readings and computers to measure changes in Earth's temperature.

_________ 4. According to the article, temperature is measured in units of horsepower.

_________ 5. Scientists have proven that the moon sends light and warmth to Earth every day of the year.

_________ 6. Reflected energy from the moon travels over 200,000 miles to reach Earth.

_________ 7. When the moon is in shadow, the temperature of Earth rises slightly.

_________ 8. The energy reflected from the moon to Earth has caused serious weather problems.

_________ 9. It takes the moon about a month to circle Earth.

_________ 10. Earth can heat the surface of the moon to temperatures as high as 200 degrees.

_________ **Bonus:** Earth gets about the same amount of energy from the sun as it gets from the moon.

The Mighty Moon

Besides slightly affecting temperature, the moon causes the ocean's surface to rise and fall. Find the tide chart in the weather section of your local newspaper. What information is listed? Look in an encyclopedia to find out more about tides.

Ducks' Sleep Habits Studied

TERRE HAUTE, Indiana (AP) — Researchers say ducks are capable of what teachers and bosses have suspected of the rest of us—sleeping with one eye open.

After putting their ducks in a row and videotaping them, researchers found mallards on the end of each row spent more time asleep with one eye open, apparently looking for predators.

The more the ducks felt threatened, the more they slept with one eye open, said lead author Niles C. Rattenborg, a graduate student at Indiana State University, Terre Haute.

"The unique aspect is not that they do it, but that they control it," Rattenborg said. "When they sleep at the edge of a group they tend to perceive greater risk, so they spend more time sleeping with one half of their brain."

Ducks with one eye open were still awake enough to detect predators, said the authors of the study, which appeared in the journal *Nature*.

Researchers studied four groups of four ducks held in plastic boxes, which were arranged in a row. Ducks on the end were found to sleep with one eye open 31.8 percent of the time, compared to 12.4 percent of the time for ducks in the central positions.

Also, ducks in the center did not open one eye more than the other, while ducks on each end kept the eye facing away from the group open 86.2 percent of the time.

Brainwave readings of the ducks showed that the half of the brain receiving signals from the closed eye indicated that half of the brain was sleeping. Signals from the half of the brain receiving signals from the open eye showed a state between fully awake and asleep.

Rattenborg said other animals, such as dolphins and other aquatic mammals, show the ability to sleep with half their brains.

Ducks Sleep With One Eye Open

Use information from the story to answer **True** or **False** to the following statements. Write **T** or **F** on the line next to each statement.

__________ 1. Researchers at Indiana State University found that the sleep habits of ducks are similar to those of humans.

__________ 2. Niels C. Rattenborg, lead author of the study, reports that ducks watch for predators while they sleep.s

__________ 3. Four groups of ducks were arranged in four rows.

__________ 4. The scientists tape-recorded the mallards (wild ducks) while they slept.

__________ 5. It was discovered that the swimming birds were able to sleep with one eye open.

__________ 6. Rattenborg found that the ducks in the center of the row slept about 12 percent longer than the ones on the end.

__________ 7. Mallards at the edge of the group behave as if they are in greater danger than ducks in the central position.

__________ 8. Ducks feeling the most risk spend the most time sleeping with one eye open.

__________ 9. By looking at brainwaves, scientists determined that ducks have half a brain.

__________ 10. According to the story, dolphins and other aquatic animals never close their eyes when they sleep.

__________ **Bonus:** It is most likely that the 16 ducks were placed in plastic boxes to keep them safe from harm.

Time to Calculate

Do some research of your own. How much time do you spend during a weekday on the activities listed below? Record the number of hours you devote to each thing. Then convert each answer to a percent. (Hint: One hour equals about four percent of a day.) What other daily activities could you add to the list?

- eating
- chores
- homework
- sleeping
- watching TV

Professor Makes Calendar of Stones

AMHERST, Mass. (AP) — Even with powerful earth-moving machines, it isn't easy to build a calendar of standing stones to mark the seasons.

But using an ancient design and 56 tons of Berkshire granite, Judith Young has created a teaching tool for a new millennium with her massive modern stone circle. It sits outside the football stadium at the University of Massachusetts.

The rough granite blocks are labeled to mark the rising and setting of the sun on the solstices and equinox, as well as the extremes of moonrise and moonset.

Young's sun wheel, a stone circle 130 feet in diameter, has evolved over the past six years. It is no mere replica of Stonehenge, the 4,000-year-old stone circle that rises from Britain's Salisbury Plain, aligned along the rising of the sun at the summer solstice.

Her standing stones are precisely aligned to Amherst's latitude to allow university students, schoolchildren and just ordinary folks to explore the mysteries of the universe.

"It's a way to teach people about the sky and to love science and the universe without using electricity or computers," said Young, an astronomy professor who has developed special lessons for middle and elementary school teachers using the sun wheel.

"This isn't something you find in a book," she said. "It was the first science."

The most popular times for visitors—about 3,000 have visited in the last year—are the midsummer and midwinter days. The solstices mark the times when, because of Earth's 23.5-degree tilt, the sun's path seems farthest from the equator. In the Northern Hemisphere, the summer solstice, June 21, is the longest day; the winter solstice, December 21, is the shortest day.

On a winter afternoon with dark shadows stretching across the great stones and the frost-seared grasses in a field outside the football stadium, it's easy to understand why the solstices were so important to ancient civilizations.

"The word *solstice* means the 'stand still,'" Young said. "For two weeks around the summer and winter solstice the sun appears to stand still—rise and set in the same spot. They couldn't miss it."

 ©Teacher Created Resources, Inc.

Ancient Calendar Marks the Seasons

Use information from the story to answer **True** or **False** to the following statements. Write **T** or **F** on the line next to each statement.

__________ 1. Astronomer Judith Young built an ancient calendar of tall standing stones at the University of Massachusetts.

__________ 2. Young's sun wheel is an exact copy of Stonehenge, a 4,000-year-old stone circle built in England.

__________ 3. Each of the calendar's massive blocks of granite measures 130 feet in diameter.

__________ 4. The rough stones are labeled to show the rising and setting of the sun at different times during the year.

__________ 5. The college professor uses the modern stone circle to teach schoolchildren about the sky.

__________ 6. Young finds it impossible to explore the universe without using electricity and computers.

__________ 7. Northern Hemisphere, June 21 is the day of the year with the most hours of sunlight.

__________ 8. On the winter solstice, December 21, the sun never sets.

__________ 9. Most people visit the Massachusetts campus on the equinox, when the time of day and night is equal.

__________ 10. It is likely the solstice was important to ancient civilizations because it marked the coming of a new season.

__________ **Bonus:** You can guess that the longest shadows are cast across the stones in winter because that's when the sun is lowest in the sky.

Sun Stones

There's lots more about the solar calendar on the Net at *www.umass.edu/sunwheel.* Begin by clicking on the image and then on the words "What is a Sunwheel?" Scroll down the page to see pictures of the tall stone circle. Look for differences in the photos taken at sunrise on the winter and summer solstices. Before returning to the main page, stop off at Stonehenge. It's amazing!

Researchers Unearth Ape Fossil

NEW YORK, N.Y. (AP) — Anthropologists have a new snapshot for the human family album, and she's got a face only a mother could love: gaping, squarish eyes, a protruding mouth and not much of a forehead.

But who looks attractive after being buried for 10 million years?

Ankarapithecus meteai, a 60-pound, fruit-eating ape that roamed the woodlands of central Turkey long before the evolutionary split that separated humans from chimps, actually looks pretty good to people who study human evolution.

For years they've had almost no fossil evidence of what happened to humanity's ancestors between about 18 million years ago and 5 million years ago. Finally, anthropologists excavating near Ankara, Turkey, have discovered a fossil ape face more complete than any known from that period.

"I think people are going to be very surprised when they see what this looks like," said John Kappelman, a member of the expedition that discovered the fossil last year.

Kappelman, a professor at the University of Texas at Austin, and researchers from Ankara University in Turkey, the Finnish Museum of Natural History in Helsinki, and Natural History Museum in London describe the fossil face in the journal *Nature*.

The fossil probably didn't belong to a direct ancestor of modern humans. It was more of a cousin, many times removed. But studying the face will tell anthropologists much more than they now know about the common ancestor of humans and the great apes. The great ape group includes gorillas, chimpanzees and orangutans.

"There are so few specimens that are as complete as this," said David Pilbeam of Harvard University in Cambridge, Mass. "Any additional specimen makes a significant increment in our knowledge."

The new *Ankarapithecus meteai* fossil isn't the first representative of its kind. A jawbone and lower face from the same species were collected during the 1950s in the same place where the new fossil turned up. But those bones, which appear to belong to a male of the species, are much less complete than those of the female Kappelman and his colleagues found.

The species is named for the city of Ankara, 30 miles south of the site where the fossil was found, and a geological sciences institute there. The "pithecus" part comes from the Greek word for ape.

 ©Teacher Created Resources, Inc.

Fossil Face Found

Use information from the story to answer **True** or **False** to the following statements. Write **T** or **F** on the line next to each statement.

__________ 1. Anthropologists (scientists who study human beings) uncovered the body of an ape in the woodlands of Turkey.

__________ 2. The ape, known as *Ankarapithecus meteai,* is believed to have lived 10 million years ago.

__________ 3. The species is named after a city in Greece.

__________ 4. This is the first time that researchers have excavated (dug up) bones belonging to the fruit-eating ape.

__________ 5. The new specimen is valuable because the bones belong to a female.

__________ 6. Using photographs found in a family album, experts are able to see what the fossil face once looked like.

__________ 7. John Kappelman, an expedition member, believes that the ape's protruding mouth and unusual eyes will surprise people.

__________ 8. Chimpanzees and gorillas are the only two members of the great ape group.

__________ 9. Scientists are studying the fossil so that they can learn more about the connections between humans and great apes.

__________ 10. According to the article, modern humans are probably not direct descendents of the 60-pound primate.

__________ **Bonus:** The unearthed face is particularly important because it is the most complete fossil of the species ever found.

Photo Finish

You can tell a lot about a person by looking at his or her face. Search your local paper for a picture of a face that "catches your eye." Write an essay that describes the person's features and explains why the photo interests you. What might the person be thinking?

Asian Stink Bugs Trouble for Farmers

STATE COLLEGE, Pa. (AP) — An insect that's recently made its way into the country smells like trouble for Pennsylvania farmers.

A scientist from Cornell University has identified the first infestation in the United States of Asian stink bugs, which can be harmful to crops.

The bugs were found in residential neighborhoods in Allentown, Pa.

"I was shocked to see so many of these stink bugs in and around the houses, on the siding, on the screens, on the door frames, inside windows in the garage—they were all over the place," said Richard Hoebeke, assistant curator of Cornell University Insect Collection, who helped identify the bugs.

"In fact, they were so numerous in one area that I had to brush them off my vehicle before I went back to New York state," Hoebeke said.

What Hoebeke found was the brown marmorated stink bug, named for its marmorated, or marbled, shell. The insect is native to China, Japan and South Korea. Researchers still don't know how the bug might have gotten to Pennsylvania, but Hoebeke said they might have been accidentally packed into shipping containers.

Like other stink bugs, the brown marmorated stink bug has glands that secrete a smelly substance when the insect is disturbed.

Karen Bernhard, a horticulture and entomology specialist with the county extension service, said the smell was "kind of sweet."

"I find it unpleasant, but many people calling say they never notice it," she said.

The bugs often aren't noticed in the summer. But as temperatures drop in the fall, the insects congregate where it's warm, often creeping into homes.

The stink bugs can pose a serious danger to farmers. In Asia, the species is known as a crop pest, feeding on tree fruits—with a particular affinity for Fuji apples—and some vegetables.

 ©Teacher Created Resources, Inc.

Pests from Asia Cause Stink

Use information from the story to answer **True** or **False** to the following statements. Write **T** or **F** on the line next to each statement.

__________ 1. Asian stink bugs are no longer found in China, Japan, and South Korea.

__________ 2. For the first time, large numbers of the smelly insects were discovered in upstate New York.

__________ 3. It is believed the Asian crop pest may have traveled to the United States in shipping containers.

__________ 4. According to the story, the shell of the brown bug is described as marmorated because it is the size of a marble.

__________ 5. Stink bugs produce a foul odor when bothered or annoyed.

__________ 6. Insect expert Karen Bernhard likes the bug's sweet smell.

__________ 7. The troublesome creature is a problem for Pennsylvania farmers because it feeds on fruits and vegetables.

__________ 8. Scientist Richard Hoebeke figured out that stink bugs are most often found hiding in garbage.

__________ 9. As part of his research, Hoebeke decided to count all the insects living in Allentown houses.

__________ 10. When discovered in homes, the bugs are considered more annoying than destructive.

__________ **Bonus:** After reading this story, you can guess that some people are not bothered by the smell of the Asian bug.

Smells Like Skunk!

The skunk is another animal that gives off a foul odor. Look in an encyclopedia to find out how this creature compares to the stink bug. Write a short report on what you've learned. Include information on where the skunk is found, its coloring, and its eating habits. When does it produce its offensive smell? Hope you never get "sprayed!"

Forests Expected to Yield Morels

DEARY, Idaho (AP) — Lori Carris crept through the forest, knife in hand, searching the ground for her tiny prey.

Spotting it, she dropped to one knee and slashed with the knife. The morel fell into her hand.

"Lori is the mushroom queen," said an admiring Jack Rogers, a fellow mushroom hunter in the Thatuna Hills, near Moscow.

Spring means the start of the month-long morel mushroom season in Northwest forests. Amateur and commercial pickers scour the forests, looking for the spongy fungus whose nutty taste is a complement to steaks, pizza and eggs.

Last year's big wildfires that burned six million acres in the West are expected to produce a bumper crop of morels because mushrooms thrive in recent burns. But a cold spring and drought in the Pacific Northwest have delayed the emergence of the mushrooms from the ground.

Hunting for wild mushrooms is a hobby, much like hunting, fishing or stamp collecting. Organized clubs in many cities stage weekend "forays" into the woods where prized locations are jealously guarded.

The spring season usually occurs in May. There is a fall season in October.

Of the Spokane Mushroom Club in Washington more than 100 members foray into the woods in search of mushrooms, President David Jones said.

"I've been mushrooming since I was in the first grade," Jones said.

On a sunny weekday, Rogers and Carris searched along a logging road just north of the town of Deary in the Idaho panhandle. Both are plant pathologists, but this trip was for pleasure as much as business.

Carris, who conducts research on plant diseases caused by wild fungi, loves to eat wild mushrooms, saying there's no substitute for the taste of morels in the spring or chanterelles in the fall.

Morels, prized for their texture and taste, stick out of the forest floor and look a lot like pine cones, making it easy for them to hide in plain sight.

Mushrooming is not as popular in the United States as it is in Europe, in part because people here worry they will be poisoned if they eat the wrong type, Rogers said.

Wild About Mushrooms

Use information from the story to answer **True** or **False** to the following statements. Write **T** or **F** on the line next to each statement.

__________ 1. According to the article, people who enjoy hunting for wild mushrooms also fish and collect stamps.

__________ 2. Morel mushrooms can be found in the spring in Northwest forests of North America.

__________ 3. David Jones has been president of the Spokane Mushroom Club since he was in the first grade.

__________ 4. The best places for locating morel mushrooms are in burned areas of forests.

__________ 5. This year the tiny plants appeared late in the season because of ice and rainstorms in the Pacific.

__________ 6. When Jack Rogers refers to Lori Carris as "the mushroom queen," he means she's very good at finding the fungus.

__________ 7. The spongy mushrooms are difficult to spot because they look like pine cones that have fallen to the ground.

__________ 8. The fleshy, brain-like objects are often seen creeping along the forest floor.

__________ 9. Morels have a nutty flavor that goes well with pizza.

__________ 10. Mushrooming is more popular in Europe than in the United States because Americans are sick of eating fungi.

__________ **Bonus:** You can guess that many mushroom hunters think of their forays (short trips) into the woods as an adventure.

Don't Munch on These Mushrooms!

Death cap, fly agaric, and jack-o'-lantern are the names of three deadly mushrooms. Look in an encyclopedia to find out more about these poisonous fungi. Which one glows in the dark? Which is used to kill flies? Which is found on the stumps of rotting trees? Which one is especially harmful to people? By the way, what makes these plants inedible?

Missouri Farmer Breeds Colorful Sheep

BOONESBORO, Mo. (AP) — Andy McMurry considers himself an abstract artist, but his preferred medium isn't oil paints or sculpting clay—it's sheep.

McMurry has a flock of 400 sheep that he's bred for their naturally colorful wool, ranging from hues of brown, black and white to shiny grays and even hints of blue or red.

The wool sheared from the sheep is spun into yarn and woven by McMurry's mother, Elzan McMurry, into shawls, scarfs and throws. No dyes or bleaches are used, but the natural look of the wool makes the finished product rich in color.

"The reason I got into these sheep is it's just like painting...it's totally an expression," says Andy McMurry, who also does decorative home painting.

In an agricultural field where white wool is king and sheep are more often bred for their meat, a handful of farmers raise the animals for colorful wool.

The National Colored Wool Growers Association has fewer than 650 members, many of them hobbyists with just a few dozen sheep. According to the American Sheep Industry Association, there are about 66,000 sheep producers in the United States.

McMurry, 33, developed an interest in sheep at age 19 while participating in a Future Farmers of America exchange program in 1988 in New Zealand.

When he returned home to the family farm, he arranged for a colored ram and six pregnant colored ewes to be placed on a ship carrying 2,000 otherwise white sheep headed from New Zealand to Canada. From there, McMurry brought the colored sheep to his farm near the Missouri River.

His sheep are of two breeds: Romneys, with longer-than-usual wool, and Merinos, with finer wool.

From those first seven sheep, McMurry has mixed and matched their offspring, generating new colors and textures and strengthening the bloodlines of those that he finds most appealing.

After shearing a lamb in a demonstration for visitors one fall day, McMurry rolled a handful of the soft wool over and over in his palm—a process that with soap and water can turn wool into felt. For McMurry, just feeling the wool is relaxing.

He explains how the sun has faded the warm coppery brown of the wool to a cooler grayish brown at the tips. That's what gives the wool its visual depth.

"I think it would make pretty yarn," says McMurry, envisioning a potential scarf. "The wool is so engaging to me, I just look at it, and it's, 'Wow!'"

©Teacher Created Resources, Inc.

Sheep's Wool Naturally Colorful

Use information from the story to answer **True** or **False** to the following statements. Write **T** or **F** on the line next to each statement.

__________ 1. Andy McMurry is an artist who paints pictures of strange-looking farm animals.

__________ 2. At age 19, McMurry joined a Future Farmers of America program because he was interested in selling woolen scarfs.

__________ 3. The "artistic" farmer traveled to Canada to look for red and blue sheep.

__________ 4. According to the story, most sheep are white.

__________ 5. American farmers raise about 65,000 sheep for their meat each year.

__________ 6. McMurry's flock of 400 sheep has unusual colored wool.

__________ 7. The 33-year-old Missouri farmer specializes in breeding animals for the natural color and feel of their wool.

__________ 8. Merino sheep are valued for their soft, fine wool.

__________ 9. Before spinning the wool into yarn, Elzan McMurry dyes the sheep hair shades of brown, black, and silvery gray.

__________ 10. During a shearing demonstration at his farm, McMurry told visitors that soap and water are used to turn wool into felt.

__________ **Bonus:** McMurry believes sheep breeding is like painting because he can mix and match animals to create colorful, eye-catching colors.

Farm Photos

Colorful sheep are rare. Pay a visit to the McMurry family farm at *www.genopalette.com/home.html.* Click on the word "Photos" for a look at these beautiful animals. You won't want to miss the shearing pictures. Why the name Genopalette? Select "Our Story" at the bottom of the main photo page for the answer!

Find Suggests Earliest Americas Writing

WASHINGTON, D.C. (AP) — Symbols carved on stones 2,600 years ago in Mexico suggest that the Olmecs, an early North American people, invented the first writing system in the Americas and that the symbols were adopted by later native cultures such as the Mayans.

The symbols were found on chips from a stone plaque and on a cylinder stone used for printing that were unearthed in an archaeological dig near an ancient Olmec city on the Gulf of Mexico.

"These symbols have a very close resemblance to symbols that were found from a later era among Mayan artifacts," said Kevin O. Pope, a study co-author. "We think the writing was developed by the Olmecs and then adopted later by the Mayans."

Age dating suggests the artifacts were deposited on the site around 650 B.C., about 350 years before the date of specimens previously thought to be the earliest examples of Meso-American writing.

The Olmecs are thought to have established a large and complex culture starting around 1300 B.C. They built massive pyramids, carved intricate and delicate sculpture and built large cities with thousands of people. The Olmecs are credited with creating a political state, with rulers and royalty, and a formal government.

Pope, a scientist with Geo Eco Arc Research of Maryland, said the Olmec culture collapsed by about 400 B.C., not long after the Mayan culture began to rise farther south.

Mary E.D. Pohl, first author of the study and a researcher at Florida State University, said it was known that the Olmec originated many of the cultural traditions later adopted by other cultures in the Americas. But evidence of writing was missing until now.

Pohl said the artifacts were found in a large deposit that included shards of pottery and drinking vessels, animal bones and hollow figurines. She said these items may have been discarded in a ritual associated with a feast or celebration.

The most complete specimen is a cylinder with raised carvings on the outside. The researchers think it was used as a rolling imprinting device, probably to apply the symbols to cloth or even to human skin, Pope said.

On the cylinder is a symbol of a bird, wings extended, with lines leading from the mouth to additional symbols to one side.

 ©Teacher Created Resources, Inc.

Ancient Writing System Uncovered

Use information from the story to answer **True** or **False** to the following statements. Write **T** or **F** on the line next to each statement.

__________ 1. The Olmecs were ancient people who established a culture in North America 1,300 years ago.

__________ 2. The Olmecs built huge pyramids and complex cities.

__________ 3. In about 650 B.C., the people of Mexico set up a police state ruled by royalty.

__________ 4. Researcher Mary E.D. Pohl said many of the Olmec traditions were later adopted by other native cultures.

__________ 5. Archaeologists uncovered evidence of a writing system at the site of an ancient Olmec city.

__________ 6. Before the discovery of Olmec symbols, experts believed the Mayans had created the first Meso-American writing.

__________ 7. The most complete artifact unearthed at the dig was a cylinder stone with symbols carved on the outside.

__________ 8. The Olmecs might have used the cylinder to print symbols on clothing and skin.

__________ 9. Pictures of birds found on a stone plaque don't look like symbols found on Mayan artifacts.

__________ 10. Objects discovered at the site included potato chips and sailing vessels.

__________ **Bonus:** Scientists used age dating to find out how old the Olmecs were when they began designing symbols and pictures.

The Hieroglyphic Connection

Any system of writing that use symbols to represent objects is called hieroglyphics. Egyptian hieroglyphics may be the oldest form of writing. Look in an encyclopedia to find out how the discovery of the Rosetta Stone enabled scholars to decipher Egyptian writing. Write a paragraph explaining how the mystery of hieroglyphics was solved. Where is the Rosetta Stone now?

Scientists Discover "Extinct" Tree

GLAND, Switzerland (AP) — The discovery in Mauritius of a tree believed extinct for more than a century is spurring efforts to save the species, a conservation group said.

The small tree, called the *trochetia parviflora*, had not been seen in the wild since 1863 until scientists found one clinging to a rocky slope on the Indian Ocean island nation, the World Conservation Union said.

"We could not believe we had found the species. It seemed too good to be true," Mauritian scientist Vincent Florens, who found the tree with colleague Jean-Claude Sevathian, said in a statement. "We both knew the plant very well from old herbarium samples and knew what it was immediately."

Florens described it as "exquisite," with a curvy trunk, dense branches, small pointed leaves and pale green fruit. The tree had probably survived for centuries in its cliff-edge hideaway, he said.

After finding the first tree, the scientists intensified their search on the mountain and found 62 other specimens of the same species.

Florens and Sevathian have now taken cuttings from the trees and have collected seeds to try to grow new plants to increase the wild population.

It will still be hard to preserve the tree, said Florens, who is part of a commission established by the World Conservation Union to save endangered species.

All the trees were found in a small area on the mountain slope that is vulnerable to landslides and fire, he said.

The species also faces other threats. Invasive foreign plants, brought to the island by humans, have taken over almost all its natural habitats and are choking areas where it remains. Animals brought to the island by settlers in the past also eat the tree's fruit, and the trees are frequently attacked by termites.

Mauritius has nearly 300 threatened species of plants, or around 27 percent of the island's estimated 1,100 native species.

"Now that this almost mythical species has been rediscovered, maybe we can hope that one day, people could find other 'extinct' species clinging to life in other remote areas," Florens said.

 ©Teacher Created Resources, Inc.

Island Home to "Extinct" Tree

Use information from the story to answer **True** or **False** to the following statements. Write **T** or **F** on the line next to each statement.

__________ 1. Scientists Vincent Florens and Jean-Claude Sevathian found an old tree growing out of a rock on an Indian reservation.

__________ 2. The small tree was thought to be extinct.

__________ 3. Over the last 100 years, trochetia parviflora has been seen by many people on the island of Mauritius.

__________ 4. When Florens and Sevathian first spotted the plant specimen, they were unable to identify it.

__________ 5. After searching the Indian island, the researchers discovered 62 other "extinct" species of trees.

__________ 6. Mauritius is home to 300 kinds of endangered plants.

__________ 7. The centuries-old tree is described as having lots of branches that wrap around its trunk.

__________ 8. Foreign plants and termites threaten to destroy this beautiful species.

__________ 9. Saving the species will be difficult because its habitat is often the site of landslides and fire.

__________ 10. In hopes of increasing the wild tree population, the scientists will try to grow new plants from cuttings and seeds.

__________ **Bonus:** It is likely the conservationists recognized the "extinct" tree because of its curvy trunk and pale green fruit.

Island Adventure

Imagine that you were exploring the island nation of Mauritius with Florens and Sevathian when they made their unexpected discovery. Use information from the story to write a journal entry about your amazing adventure. Decorate your page with a picture of the exquisite tree. Would you like to taste the fruit?

Chinese Use PJs for More Than Sleep

SHANGHAI, China (AP) — Zhan Chunyong likes nothing better after work than to slip into her pajamas and head out to do grocery shopping.

And the 42-year-old security guard is not the only one. It's a common sight in China's biggest, most prosperous city: men and women in public dressed as if in their bedrooms.

You can see them in their nightclothes on busy sidewalks, walking amid the business suits as if it were the most natural thing in the world. At supermarkets, they shuffle in slippers behind shopping carts. Some zip by on motor scooters, plaid flannels flapping in the wind.

Shanghainese say they've been wearing pajamas in public for at least 10 years, since the economy took off and they could afford to add sleepware to wardrobes that consisted of little more than drab gray and blue Mao suits. Far from being embarrassed, they say pajamas are more comfortable than regular clothes—especially in Shanghai's notoriously hot, sticky summers—and easier to wash. They're a luxury and a way to flaunt new wealth.

"Only people in cities can afford clothes like this. In farming villages, they still have to wear old work clothes to bed," Zhan said.

Residents seem to look on it as a charming local quirk. So do officials in charge of keeping Shanghai looking smart.

"Some say it's not civilized, but it's just a harmless habit of the residents," said Zhang Limin, a spokesman for the City Environment Supervision Office.

Many in the city of 17 million are surprised to hear people elsewhere don't parade in public in their pajamas.

"Pajamas look good and feel good. Everyone wears them outside. No one would laugh," said Wang Hui, a 17-year-old high school student in a pink nightgown decorated with a smiling kitten face. She and a friend, who was dressed in light green pajamas, were stepping out of a convenience store with canned tea and bags of potato chips.

Wang said she changes out of her school uniform as soon as she gets home. Her mother and father also put on pajamas. "I have three more summer gowns like this one. I wear a different one everyday."

Li Xiaoling, who owns a shop in central Shanghai that sells nothing but pajamas, said she could tell someone's social status with a glance at their sleepwear.

A member of the new professional class might splurge on a $12 pair, with high quality material and a stylish cut. But most Shanghainese still favor pajamas costing $2 to $3.50. Patterns and styles go in and out of fashion, just like other clothing.

 ©Teacher Created Resources, Inc.

PJs: The Height of Chinese Fashion

Use information from the story to answer **True** or **False** to the following statements. Write **T** or **F** on the line next to each statement.

__________ 1. For the past 10 years, residents of Shanghai have been wearing fancy outfits to bed.

__________ 2. Many in Shanghai go outside in pajamas because the clothes are considered both comfortable and stylish.

__________ 3. Shanghai residents are especially fond of pajamas that look like gray and blue business suits.

__________ 4. Chinese supermarkets sell a wide selection of stylish plaid and flannel sleepwear.

__________ 5. The most popular pajamas in Shanghai sell for about $3.

__________ 6. Women in China's most prosperous city are often seen grocery shopping in their nightgowns.

__________ 7. Teenagers who go to convenience stores in their school uniforms are laughed at by their friends.

__________ 8. Many in the city of 17 million are embarrassed to be seen shuffling around in their slippers.

__________ 9. In China's farming villages, residents sleep in work clothes because they cannot afford to buy pajamas.

__________ 10. Men and women who stroll through the streets of Shanghai in nightwear are thought to be wealthy.

__________ **Bonus:** Since parading around in pajamas is so popular, the Chinese are surprised people in other countries haven't tried it.

Pajama Party

If you were allowed to have a sleepover party at your house, do you think you could do it for under $25? Below is a list of items you'll need for the overnight stay. Plan on inviting five friends and figure out the cost of the party. See if you can stay within your budget. What kind of pajamas will you wear?

- two rented movies
- paper plates and cups
- popcorn
- soft drinks
- midnight snacks
- pizza

Answer Key

Vocabulary #1 (page 7)

1. i	6. e
2. f	7. b
3. c	8. d
4. h	9. j
5. g	10. a

Vocabulary #2 (page 9)

1. b	6. h
2. f	7. i
3. j	8. e
4. g	9. d
5. a	10. c

Vocabulary #3 (page 11)

1. h	6. a
2. i	7. c
3. j	8. e
4. d	9. f
5. b	10. g

Vocabulary #4 (page 13)

1. h	6. a
2. f	7. i
3. d	8. c
4. g	9. e
5. b	10. j

Vocabulary #5 (page 15)

1. f	6. j
2. g	7. a
3. c	8. b
4. d	9. h
5. e	10. i

Vocabulary #6 (page 17)

1. j	6. a
2. i	7. e
3. h	8. b
4. g	9. f
5. d	10. c

Vocabulary #7 (page 19)

1. a	6. g
2. b	7. i
3. d	8. e
4. f	9. c
5. h	10. j

Vocabulary #8 (page 21)

1. g	6. d
2. c	7. h
3. b	8. j
4. a	9. e
5. i	10. f

Vocabulary #9 (page 23)

1. c	6. h
2. d	7. g
3. e	8. f
4. i	9. a
5. j	10. b

Vocabulary #10 (page 25)

1. d	6. h
2. j	7. f
3. i	8. b
4. a	9. g
5. e	10. c

Vocabulary #11 (page 27)

1. e	6. i
2. g	7. j
3. h	8. a
4. b	9. c
5. d	10. f

Vocabulary #12 (page 29)

1. f	6. j
2. c	7. g
3. b	8. i
4. d	9. h
5. e	10. a

Vocabulary #13 (page 31)

1. g	6. b
2. f	7. i
3. e	8. c
4. a	9. j
5. h	10. d

Vocabulary #14 (page 33)

1. e	6. i
2. f	7. j
3. g	8. b
4. a	9. c
5. h	10. d

Vocabulary #15 (page 35)

1. c	6. i
2. h	7. d
3. a	8. g
4. j	9. e
5. b	10. f

Vocabulary #16 (page 37)

1. e	6. b
2. h	7. g
3. a	8. c
4. d	9. i
5. j	10. f

Q and A #1 (page 41)

1. Answers will vary.
2. The *Tyrannosaurus rex* exhibit now includes the smell of the dinosaur's habitat.
3. T-rex's awful smell could have come from the blood of its prey, eating bad meat, or infected wounds.
4. The killer beast attacked duckbilled dinosaurs, triceratops and other plant-eating creatures.
5. Answers will vary.
6. The authentic smell of the dinosaur was thought to be so off-putting (unpleasant) that it might disgust people.
7. Horner says the dinosaur was the worst, most foul-smelling animal that ever lived.
8. The dinosaur's environment has a boggy (marshy), acrid, earthy scent.
9. Answers will vary.
10. Answers will vary.

Q and A #2 (page 43)

1. The Japanese government is planning to change the school schedule by giving children extra days off.
2. Children go to school about 6 days a week in Japan.
3. Japanese children attend school about 60 more days a year than American children.
4. The Education Ministry decides the length of the school year.
5. Mitsuo Arai is opposed to a shorter week because he feels that the students will not have enough time to learn all the material he must teach.
6. If the plan goes into effect, the number of hours the children have to spend in class will not change.
7. Answer will vary.
8. To make up for lost time, the children might have to spend less time on sports, activities, or free time.
9. Answers will vary.
10. Answers will vary.

Q and A #3 (page 45)

1. Researchers found a giant ant colony stretching along the coast of Italy to northwest Spain.
2. The 3,600-mile supercolony consists of billions of Argentine ants.
3. Before seeing the report, Fell thought the largest colonies of Argentine ants were a few city blocks long.
4. Answers will vary.
5. Keller thinks the ants were accidently brought into Europe around 1920 in ships carrying plants.
6. The colony is called cooperative because ants from different nests do not fight with each other.
7. Researchers think the ants are cooperative because they recognize their genetic relationship.
8. A smaller supercolony was found in the Catalonia region of Spain.
9. When ants from the two supercolonies came in contact with each other, they fought to the death.
10. Answers will vary.

Q and A #4 (page 47)

1. The Great Stone Face was formed by a series of geologic events that began 200 million years ago.
2. Answers will vary.
3. For the past century, stabilizing cables and epoxy were used to prevent the granite symbol from weakening.
4. Answers will vary.
5. Pelchat thinks the combination of heavy rains, high winds, and freezing temperatures caused the rock to fall.

©Teacher Created Resources, Inc.

Answer Key *(cont.)*

6. It is unclear when the actual collapse occurred because clouds covered the mountain at the time of the fall.
7. The face appears on the state quarter, road signs, and many souvenirs and tourist booklets.
8. Daniel Webster was a 19th-century New Hampshire statesman. He wrote that the Old Man was a sign that God makes men.
9. Answers will vary.
10. Answers will vary.

Q and A #5 (page 49)

1. About 27 million children receive school meals each day.
2. Schools are serving students healthier food in an effort to meet the requirements of federal officials.
3. The Agriculture Department conducted the last survey during the 1998-99 school year.
4. In 1991, a third of all elementary schools in the United States provided students with low-fat meals.
5. Answers will vary.
6. Schools have trimmed fat, cholesterol and sodium from the food they serve.
7. The Agricultural Department recommends a maximum of 30 percent of calories from fat.
8. Answers will vary.
9. Answers will vary.
10. Answers will vary.

Q and A #6 (page 51)

1. The Dominican Republic's Beata Island is located in the Caribbean Sea.
2. Beata is isolated because it takes 5 hours by boat to reach the island.
3. Answers will vary.
4. Answers will vary.
5. The Jaragua gecko measures 1.6 centimeters.
6. The dark brown lizard has soft skin, a stout body, and suction pads on its feet.
7. Answers will vary.
8. Scientists think the lizard eats small ants, spiders, and soil-dwelling mites.
9. The lizard, known as *Sphaerodactylus ariasae*, was named after biologist Yvonne Arias.
10. Answers will vary.

Q and A #7 (page 53)

1. Olowe of Ise produced wood carvings. He worked for kings of the Yoruba people.
2. When the African sculptor was in his 20s, he was a messenger in the king's court.
3. It is not known how Olowe learned his woodcarving skill.
4. Answers will vary.
5. It is difficult to prove that the artist carved by feel because there are so few written accounts of his work.
6. Answers will vary.
7. Olowe created figures, columns, and doors for African palaces.
8. Answers will vary.
9. The curator of the one-man show is Roslyn A. Walker. Olowe's work was displayed at the National Museum of African Art in Washington, D.C.
10. Answers will vary.

Q and A #8 (page 55)

1. All kinds of bugs are on view at the Insectarium.
2. Answers will vary.
3. Kanya decided to open a museum after he noticed that children liked to look at his catches of dead creatures.
4. In the Insectarium, dead insects are mounted (set for display) on the walls.
5. The museum is showing off bugs that look like leaves and ornate (fancy) insects that are worn as jewelry.
6. People touring the museum may touch dead bugs from Africa, Asia, and Australia.
7. Answers will vary.
8. Millipedes are a vital (important) part of the ecosystem because they make space in dirt for plants to grow.
9. Answers will vary.
10. Answers will vary.

Q and A #9 (page 57)

1. Post-it Notes are little pieces of paper with adhesive on the back. 3M began selling them in 1980.
2. Answers will vary.
3. The original Post-it Notes were square and came in bright yellow.
4. Fry used slips of paper to keep his place in the hymnbook, but the bookmarks kept falling out.
5. Spencer's adhesive was unusual because it could be repositioned.
6. Answers will vary.
7. After placing a note on a report intended for a fellow worker, Fry realized he had found a new way to send messages.
8. Answers will vary.
9. Answers will vary.
10. The scientist is most pleased with the fact that so many people use and appreciate his invention.

Q and A #10 (page 59)

1. Stalagmites are formed by the slow dripping of mineral water from the roof of a cave.
2. The stalagmites used in Polyak's research were taken from Carlsbad Caverns and two other caves.
3. Scientists studied the cone-shaped columns of stone by cutting them into thin sections.
4. The rings of calcite remind Polyak of the growth rings found in trees.
5. During the drier years, thin bands of calcite formed. During the wet years, thicker rings formed.
6. Answers will vary.
7. Answers will vary.
8. The fact that the stalagmites have not grown for the past 700 years indicates the beginning of a dry period for New Mexico that continues to this day.
9. Answers will vary.
10. About 1,000 years ago, the Pueblo made their homes in the mountains. Today they live in river valleys.

Q and A #11 (page 61)

1. The largest flower in the world bloomed in London's Kew Gardens.
2. Titan arum is 10 feet tall. It is found in the rain forests of Sumatra, Indonesia.
3. The last time the flower bloomed was in 1963.
4. Austin and his friends wore masks because they expected the gigantic plant to have a very bad odor.
5. Boyce thinks that the scent of the flower is similar to rotting flesh or to a rubbish bin in the summer.
6. Answers will vary.
7. The aroma of the blossom attracts the sweat bee.
8. A few days before the petals opened, the plant grew between four and six inches a day.
9. The flower is probably very beautiful because it is bell-shaped and deep red in color.
10. Answers will vary.

Q and A #12 (page 63)

1. Researchers have discovered that dolphins are able to learn and repeat signals from their companions.
2. Analysis of more than 1,700 whistle signals took place along the Moray Firth coast of Scotland.
3. It takes just a few seconds for bottlenose dolphins to match each other's whistle.
4. Like dolphins, parrots have the ability to copy sounds.
5. Before using a spoken language, it is believed ancient humans communicated with matching signals.

Answer Key *(cont.)*

6. Answers will vary.
7. When dolphins adopt a signature whistle pattern, they "name" themselves by creating their own special signals.
8. Dolphins may use signature whistles to communicate with a specific member of their group.
9. Answers will vary.
10. Answers will vary.

Q and A #13 (page 65)

1. Clarke found a 3.3-million-year-old skeleton in a cave in South Africa.
2. The creature, scientifically known as *Australopithecus africanus*, is 4 feet tall.
3. Scientists think that the human ancestor lived both on the ground and in trees.
4. It is believed that the creature died after falling down a 45-foot shaft.
5. Before uncovering an arm and hand, Clarke had found the ape man's skull, leg bones, and pieces of his foot and ankle.
6. Hand bones of the skeleton show that "Little Foot" did not walk on his knuckles.
7. Answers will vary.
8. The ape man had fingers that curved and a thumb that was stronger than that of a modern man.
9. Answers will vary.
10. Answers will vary.

Q and A #14 (page 67)

1. Culture is the ability to learn new habits and to pass them along to future generations.
2. Researchers now believe apes may have developed culture 14 million years ago.
3. Nine primate scientists studied the results of years of observations of the orangutan.
4. Experts believe the reddish-brown primates are able to learn new behaviors and teach them to their offspring.
5. Orangutan culture is practiced independently by different groups of apes in Borneo and Sumatra.
6. Answers will vary.
7. Air is blown out through tightly-squeezed lips to make a raspberry noise and drawn in to make a kiss-squeak.
8. Answers will vary.
9. Human societies develop their own types of music, architecture, language, clothing, and art.
10. Answers will vary.

Q and A #15 (page 69)

1. Michael J. O'Brien is an anthropologist (scientist who studies human beings).
2. O'Brien has analyzed 35 samples of ancient sandals.
3. The prehistoric shoes were found in a Missouri cave. They were recovered 40 years ago.
4. The words *fashionable, tough,* and *well-made* are used to describe the old shoes.
5. The leather moccasin is thought to be 1,000 years old. It was probably made for a child.
6. Cave dwellers wove fibrous material into a tough fabric that was used to make the long-lasting footwear.
7. Prehistoric Americans needed durable shoes because the jobs they did, such as hunting for food and hauling water back to their homes, required a lot of walking.
8. Answers will vary.
9. Answers will vary.
10. Answers will vary.

Q and A #16 (page 71)

1. Researchers have wondered how it is possible for such small animals to make so much noise.
2. In the third paragraph, snapping shrimp are described as, "...2-inch-long creatures equipped with a small claw and a huge, outsized claw almost half the animal's length."
3. The puzzle was solved by a group of European scientists.
4. Answers will vary.
5. Answers will vary.
6. When a claw closes rapidly, a water jet forms, causing a drop in water pressure and the formation of a bubble.
7. The 1/8-inch bubble lasts for 700 microseconds or 700-millionths of a second.
8. When the bubble collapses, it makes a sharp clicking sound, and it creates a shock wave.
9. The animal gets its food by stunning worms and other prey with a shock wave.
10. Answers will vary.

Multiple Choice #1 (page 75)

1. a	6. c
2. a	7. c
3. b	8. a
4. b	9. b
5. a	10. c

Multiple Choice #2 (page 77)

1. a	6. b
2. c	7. b
3. a	8. a
4. c	9. c
5. a	10. c

Multiple Choice #3 (page 79)

1. a	6. b
2. b	7. a
3. c	8. b
4. b	9. c
5. c	10. b

Multiple Choice #4 (page 81)

1. b	6. b
2. c	7. b
3. b	8. c
4. a	9. a
5. a	10. b

Multiple Choice #5 (page 83)

1. b	6. a
2. c	7. c
3. c	8. a
4. b	9. b
5. b	10. c

Multiple Choice #6 (page 85)

1. b	6. a
2. c	7. b
3. c	8. c
4. a	9. a
5. a	10. a

Multiple Choice #7 (page 87)

1. b	6. c
2. a	7. c
3. b	8. a
4. c	9. c
5. b	10. b

Multiple Choice #8 (page 89)

1. b	6. a
2. a	7. a
3. c	8. c
4. b	9. c
5. b	10. c

Multiple Choice #9 (page 91)

1. a	6. b
2. a	7. c
3. c	8. b
4. c	9. a
5. a	10. c

Multiple Choice #10 (page 93)

1. c	6. b
2. a	7. a
3. c	8. c
4. b	9. a
5. c	10. b

Multiple Choice #11 (page 95)

1. c	6. b
2. b	7. c
3. c	8. b
4. a	9. c
5. c	10. a

Multiple Choice #12 (page 97)

1. c	6. a
2. a	7. a
3. a	8. c
4. b	9. c
5. b	10. b

Answer Key *(cont.)*

Multiple Choice #13 (page 99)

1. a
2. b
3. c
4. a
5. c
6. b
7. a
8. c
9. b
10. b

Multiple Choice #14 (page 101)

1. b
2. c
3. c
4. a
5. c
6. a
7. c
8. b
9. c
10. b

Multiple Choice #15 (page 103)

1. b
2. a
3. c
4. b
5. b
6. b
7. a
8. c
9. c
10. a

Multiple Choice #16 (page 105)

1. a
2. a
3. b
4. c
5. c
6. c
7. b
8. a
9. b
10. c

True or False #1 (page 109)

1. F
2. T
3. T
4. F
5. T
6. F
7. T
8. F
9. T
10. F

Bonus: F

True or False #2 (page 111)

1. T
2. F
3. F
4. T
5. F
6. F
7. T
8. F
9. F
10. T

Bonus: T

True or False #3 (page 113)

1. T
2. F
3. F
4. T
5. T
6. F
7. T
8. F
9. F
10. T

Bonus: F

True or False #4 (page 115)

1. T
2. T
3. F
4. F
5. F
6. T
7. F
8. T
9. T
10. T

Bonus: T

True or False #5 (page 117)

1. T
2. T
3. F
4. T
5. F
6. F
7. T
8. T
9. F
10. F

Bonus: T

True or False #6 (page 119)

1. T
2. F
3. F
4. T
5. F
6. T
7. F
8. T
9. F
10. T

Bonus: T

True or False #7 (page 121)

1. F
2. T
3. T
4. F
5. F
6. T
7. F
8. F
9. T
10. F

Bonus: F

True or False #8 (page 123)

1. F
2. T
3. F
4. F
5. T
6. F
7. T
8. T
9. F
10. F

Bonus: F

True or False #9 (page 125)

1. T
2. F
3. F
4. T
5. T
6. F
7. T
8. F
9. F
10. T

Bonus: T

True or False #10 (page 127)

1. F
2. T
3. F
4. F
5. F
6. F
7. T
8. F
9. T
10. T

Bonus: T

True or False #11 (page 129)

1. F
2. F
3. T
4. F
5. T
6. F
7. T
8. F
9. F
10. T

Bonus: T

True or False #12 (page 131)

1. F
2. T
3. F
4. T
5. F
6. T
7. T
8. F
9. T
10. F

Bonus: T

True or False #13 (page 133)

1. F
2. F
3. F
4. T
5. F
6. T
7. T
8. T
9. F
10. T

Bonus: T

True or False #14 (page 135)

1. F
2. T
3. F
4. T
5. T
6. T
7. T
8. T
9. F
10. F

Bonus: F

True or False #15 (page 137)

1. F
2. T
3. F
4. F
5. F
6. T
7. F
8. T
9. T
10. T

Bonus: T

True or False #16 (page 139)

1. F
2. T
3. F
4. F
5. T
6. T
7. F
8. F
9. T
10. T

Bonus: T

Progress Plotter

Name: ____

In the boxes below, record a grade for each exercise completed.

	Vocabulary	Questions and Answers	Multiple Choice	True or False
1.				
2.				
3.				
4.				
5.				
6.				
7.				
8.				
9.				
10.				
11.				
12.				
13.				
14.				
15.				
16.				

 ©Teacher Created Resources, Inc.